CRIMINAL INTERROGATION

ABOUT THE AUTHOR

Warren D. Holmes was a member of the Miami, Florida Police Department from 1951 to 1963. He was assigned to the Lie Detection Bureau from 1955 to 1963 and then left the police department to open a private polygraph testing firm. Mr. Holmes is the past president of Florida Polygraph Association and the Academy for Scientific Interrogation (the predecessor name of the American Polygraph Association).

Mr. Holmes has lectured about criminal interrogation in many organizations including the FBI, CIA, The Secret Service, Canadian Police College and the Singapore Police Department.

Mr. Holmes has conducted polygraph examinations in many nationally known cases such as the assassination of President John F. Kennedy, the murder of Dr. Martin Luther King, Jr. and Watergate.

CRIMINAL INTERROGATION

A Modern Format for Interrogating Criminal
Suspects Based on the Intellectual Approach

By

WARREN D. HOLMES

CHARLES C THOMAS • PUBLISHER, LTD.
Springfield • Illinois • U.S.A.

Published and Distributed Throughout the World by

CHARLES C THOMAS • PUBLISHER, LTD.
2600 South First Street
Springfield, Illinois 62794-9265

©2002 by CHARLES C THOMAS • PUBLISHER, LTD.

ISBN 0-398-07319-8 (hard)
ISBN 0-398-07320-1 (paper)

Library of Congress Catalog Card Number: 2002022520

*With THOMAS BOOKS careful attention is given to all details of manufacturing
and design. It is the Publisher's desire to present books that are satisfactory as to their
physical qualities and artistic possibilities and appropriate for their particular use.
THOMAS BOOKS will be true to those laws of quality that assure a good name
and good will.*

*Printed in the United States of America
TH-R-3*

Library of Congress Cataloging-in-Publication Data

Holmes, Warren D.
    Criminal interrogation : a modern format for interrogating criminal suspects based on
    the intellectual approach / by Warren D. Holmes.
        p. cm.
    ISBN 0-398-07319-8 (hard : alk. paper) – ISBN 0-398-07320-1 (pbk. : alk. paper)
    1. Police questioning. 2. Interviewing in law enforcement. I. Title.

HV8073 .H625 2002
363.25'4--dc21
                                                                        2002022520

This book is dedicated to Miami Herald *Editor, Gene Miller, my partner in the pursuit of truth, who made it possible in three different cases to free four people who were wrongly convicted of first-degree murder.*

Special thanks to my daughter, Debra Holmes, whose technical skills were a major contribution to this book.

FOREWORD

A newspaper reporter telephoned Warren D. Holmes shortly after the Ocean Drive sidewalk assassination of designer Gianni Versace on Miami Beach in 1997. What did he know about serial killers? Quite a bit, it turned out. At the end of the interview, the reporter asked casually how many homicide cases has had worked. Oh, "hundreds," Holmes replied. The next morning he read "scores." A skeptical editor had lowered it. Only then did Holmes have his secretary count–by name, date and report–homicides he'd investigated. Although few records survive from his 12 years with the Miami Police Department (maybe 400 cases), he'd kept an accurate account for his private practice. At publication of this book in 2002, that number had hit 537. And he is still counting. Perhaps no man in America has confronted as many murder suspects as Holmes. There is a reason for it. He is a superb interrogator. He gets killers to tell the truth. He obtains confessions. The confessions are valid. They are very damn thorough. "A surgeon doesn't take out half a cancer," he tells defendants.

Left uncounted here–in a career that began in 1951–are thousands of other suspects in non-lethal crimes: thieves, bank robbers, hoodlums, embezzlers, rapists, arsonists, scam artists, politicians on-the-take, drug lords, crooked cops, computer hackers, purse snatchers, shoplifters, and in general, people in trouble; some innocent bystanders, some guilty bystanders, some wrong-place-wrong time unfortunates, and other mere observers (or voyeurs) of the human condition. Aren't we all?

The opus here qualifies as a how-to book, and extremely unusual one. Specific arguments for incest suspects? Well, here they are. Murders that look like accidents? Got 'em. The topic is interrogation. . .not the polygraph. . .and it begins with the sad realization that 85 percent of criminal defendants lie to their own attorneys.

In a classic understatement, Holmes explains that people don't confess to interrogators they don't respect. That is a crucial key. In the interrogation room, Holmes is strictly business with a pure no-nonsense formality. That doesn't mean he can't be ingratiating and charming, for he is, but his success emanates from force of personality. He is inquisitive, incredibly persistent, ruthlessly logical, and when necessary, quite sympathetic.

Wrongdoers, he declares, like to hear that despite the act committed, they are not all that evil. Provocation, rather than their character, prompted the act. "One of my favorite arguments is to point out there are certain life forces so powerful that no rational thought process can control them. Anger is one. At times, we are all victims of anger."

And then, almost always, he asks a couple of final questions. "What have I forgotten to ask you?" Then, "Do you have any knowledge of any unsolved homicides?" Sometimes, the answers are real shockers.

Along the way, over the years, Holmes worked cases not easily forgotten: the John F. Kennedy assassination, Martin Luther King assassination, Watergate, financier Robert Vesco, Philadelphia mayor Frank Rizzo, the William Kennedy Smith rape allegation, and the Pitts and Lee malfunction of justice.

As a reporter and editor at *The Miami Herald,* I've labored with Holmes on-and-off for 40 years. Twice I've received the Pulitzer Prize for reporting where Holmes helped prove that defendants were wrongly convicted of murder. The jury doesn't give awards for criminal interrogation. It should.

GENE MILLER
Miami, Florida
February 22, 2002

PREFACE

For a number of years, I put aside writing this book. I was concerned that any book written about criminal interrogation exposes the author to the naïve, to the technicians of the law who are quick to find fault, and to those individuals who believe that all police interrogation should be outlawed.

I was also concerned that I would be writing about a subject so difficult that no nation has created an ideal system of criminal interrogation fair to the suspect, but with sufficient latitude for the police to determine proof. This failure is evident by the number of nations that employ torture instead of reasonable methods of inquiry.

I finally reached the conclusion that despite the inherent problems writing about criminal interrogation, I would assume the risk, hoping that what I have to say will be beneficial to the less experienced interrogator. In my opinion, there will always be debate as to the moral and legal implications of what transpires in any criminal interrogation session. In view of that fact, it is my intention to simply tell you what I think you should do and say as an interrogator to get the job done. The contents of this book are empirically-based, and I believe this is an honest reflection of my life experience as a polygraph examiner.

In retrospect, it is my opinion that the inherent difficulty in criminal interrogation is manifested by the margin of error in perceiving guilt or innocence and the length of time it takes an average person to become sufficiently experienced to reach an acceptable degree of proficiency.

Ideally, to learn how to interrogate, one should be exposed to talented interrogators in action. Any book about criminal interrogation cannot be a complete substitute for the daily or weekly experience of interrogating criminal suspects.

Recognizing that fact, it was my plan to write a "how to" book which I hoped would provide a framework for enhancing one's personal experience.

The scope of this book includes a step-by-step procedure for interrogation from the moment the suspect enters the interrogation room to the time he leaves.

One of my primary purposes in writing this book was to answer a complaint I hear most often when I lecture, "Mr. Holmes, I always run out of things to say to a suspect." To answer that complaint, I have provided suggested interrogational arguments for specific crimes.

When you finish reading this book, I hope you have one predominate thought, "you don't obtain confessions by asking the suspect questions. You have to convince a suspect to confess by the use of persuasive interrogational arguments."

W.D.H.

INTRODUCTION

The Problem: Deception as a Tool of Evolution

Mankind's effort to determine absolute human truth has been a dismal failure. There is a simple reason for this, human beings are much more proficient at lying than at detecting lies. Deception has been around a lot longer than truth-telling. In fact, telling the truth was not really needed until man started to band together; to form social groups; then the truth was needed for the administration of public affairs. Deception is the counterbalance to aggression, which is the fuel of evolution. Deception is used to enhance and cope with aggression. It is ironic that the species that have survived and prospered through the process of evolution are those that have mastered the art of deception. Both predator and prey depend upon it.

Early man apparently became so frustrated trying to determine human truth that he turned the job over to the Gods. Thus, trial by ordeal and combat came into being. It was deduced that if a person survived or was victorious in combat, he must have had the Gods on his side and therefore was truthful as well. It soon became apparent that some guilty people were escaping their just desserts. So torture became the most popular means of getting confessions with an accompanying assumption of truth. Both the state and the church condoned the use of torture. In fact, the state actually prescribed rules for the administration of the torture. To this day, torture is used in most countries to obtain confessions. The problem with torture, besides being atavistic in nature, is that it may produce a confession from a person with a low pain threshold, and you still won't know if you have obtained the truth.

As the rule of law evolved, as a natural consequence, so did the concept of an adversarial judicial system. The underlying premise of the judicial system is that the truth would emerge out of a clash between combatants in the court of law. Unfortunately, legal truth and the absolute human truth are too frequently different. An adjunct to the judicial system, law enforcement agencies developed exotic means to determine human truth through the use of hypnosis, truth serum, and the polygraph. I've used all three and they all have limitations. In my opinion, the polygraph has the fewest.

Thus far, no one has solved the problem of obtaining absolute human truth nor has anyone developed an ideal format for achieving it. When an interrogator sits across a desk from a criminal suspect, he is looking at the by-product of thousands of years of evolution. The suspect's greatest striving in life has been to protect his ego. His only interest is self-interest. Often you know he is guilty, but he is such a good liar that he can make you doubt your own mind. This book will give you the tools to combat this formidable adversary and to attain the most satisfying outcome of criminal investigation; obtaining a confession through astute interrogation.

CONTENTS

CRIMINAL INTERROGATION

Chapter I

CASE ANALYSIS

All criminal interrogations should begin with case analysis. The facts contained in offense reports, supplemental reports, witness testimony, lab reports and the input from fellow investigators help the interrogator formulate an approach before the suspect even enters the Interrogation Room. Case analysis will reveal a possible motive and give insight into the personality of the perpetrator. Case analysis often reveals whether or not the suspect is the common denominator in similar crimes, whether the crime was a planned or spontaneous act and whether the evidence against the suspect is physical, direct or circumstantial.

Case analysis helps the interrogator formulate a theory as to how the crime was committed. This theory then becomes the format for questioning. Case analysis will often reveal a mitigating factor that the interrogator can use to help the perpetrator rationalize his act and prompt him to tell the truth.

The interrogator should be a master detective and know the probative value of most evidence. He should know the danger of drawing conclusions too quickly and that the only opinion that counts is his last one. Of the people involved in the judicial system, the interrogator has the best opportunity to determine what actually occurred at the time of the crime. He deals with the suspect on a one-on-one basis in a controlled environment. The interrogator has all of the evidence at his disposal. He can talk to witnesses who are sometimes unavailable to the defense. The interrogator has the resources of his department to back him up. He should represent the old Eastern Airlines' slogan; "There is no substitute for experience."

As the person with the best shot at determining guilt or innocence, the interrogator also has the attendant liability of holding the suspect's fate in his hands. In all of the miscarriage of justice cases that I have worked on and studied, the mistakes made in those cases were initiated at the level of the lead investigator and interrogator. Those mistakes were then compounded by naive prosecutors who had no police experience.

We all know the danger of becoming married to a theory. In the pursuit of truth, ego is an insidious, undermining influence. When an interrogator becomes married to a theory, he risks ignoring all contrary evidence or indications that he could be wrong. Over the years I have learned from the mistakes I have made to be more objective and not to take things for granted. In time, the experienced interrogator learns the margin of error in witness identification, forensic lab reports and expert testimony. In the past, I have been terribly misled by reports on back-typing of blood, hair comparisons and handwriting analysis.

I once interrogated a murder suspect for more hours than I should have. I was convinced of his guilt based on the ballistics report. The exasperated suspect finally looked at me and said, "Tell me what you want me to say and I'll say it." I knew then that something was wrong. I suggested that the investigator take the suspect's gun and have it tested in another department. Their report indicated that the suspect's gun was not the murder weapon. I had placed so much faith in the initial ballistics report, that I had ignored my own polygraph test results.

The largest margin of error in the American Criminal Justice System is caused by faulty witness identification. An experienced interrogator should know not to automatically assume guilt just because the suspect has been identified. There are several reasons mistakes are made in witness identification.

1. Someone is apprehended in the vicinity of the crime who fits the general description of the culprit.
2. Since the police have the person in custody, the witness goes along assuming the police know best and have the right suspect.
3. The identification is made to provide closure.
4. The identification is made to satisfy the instinct for revenge.
5. The witness fears alienating the police or appearing stupid by admitting doubt.
6. Poor lighting at the scene.

7. The witness has poor eyesight.
8. The influence of drugs or alcohol.
9. The lineup is deliberately skewed toward a particular suspect.
10. The trauma of the crime alters the witness's perception.
11. Insufficient time is allotted to view the suspect.
12. The identification is biased by overemphasis on a single character-
    istic such as eyes, voice, or item of clothing.

Many people are convicted based on perjured identifications. A victim or witness will deliberately identify the wrong person to protect someone else. They will do this out of fear or revenge or to divert the attention of the police away from themselves or someone they are protecting. It is difficult to conceive that someone would frame an innocent person by making a false identification but it's done often by someone who wants to get out of jail or get his sentence reduced. Professional snitches often dupe both the police and the prosecutors. They have become a national problem. Most professional snitches are psychopaths, drug addicts and alcoholics. Mainly, they are prolific liars.

Any testimony induced by hypnosis should be suspect. In the 1950s and 1960s, hypnosis became a new tool for the police. In Florida, the use of hypnosis in criminal cases caused so many problems that now such testimony is prohibited.

Many years ago, I worked on a case where two Black men were convicted and sentenced to death for killing two gas station attendants. Several years after their conviction, I got a confession from the man who actually killed the two attendants. During a motion for a new trial, the judge allowed a key witness against the two Black men to be hypnotized in court. Under hypnosis, she testified she saw the two Black men commit the killings. She put on a great act and duped the judge who denied a new trial. Eventually, after a team put in years of work on their behalf, the two Black men were pardoned and received compensation from the State of Florida for their wrongful convictions. This case taught me firsthand how dangerous testimony induced by hypnosis can be.

Recently, I worked on a case where a man was sentenced to death based primarily on the testimony of a juvenile who had been hypnotized and subsequently testified against the defendant. The inmate was scheduled to die in the electric chair in nine days when I was asked to review the trial transcript. I became convinced the juvenile had lied.

I suggested to the *Miami Herald* that they investigate the case. They assigned reporter Lori Roza to interview the witness, now a grown man. He confessed to Lori Roza that he had made up his hypnosis-induced testimony. The Florida State Supreme Court stopped the execution and ordered a hearing to determine if a new trial was in order. The state agreed not to retry the inmate.

The interrogator should be aware that some terrible injustices have occurred in cases in which a suspect has been accused of being a serial killer or rapist. This happens as follows; the suspect is linked to some of the crimes because of witness identification. Then, despite airtight alibis, he is also accused of other crimes with a similar MO. The police explain away the alibis by attributing some of the crimes to copycat criminals. It has been my experience that reliance on witness identification should never supercede the importance of MO in targeting a suspect. A similar MO is generally characteristic of the same suspect.

I was one of three polygraph examiners selected by the Attorney General of the State of Massachusetts to administer a polygraph test to Albert De Salvo, "The Boston Strangler." The other examiners were Charles Zimmerman and John Reid. De Salvo confessed to noted Attorney, F. Lee Bailey, that he was "The Boston Strangler." In my opinion, he gave Attorney Bailey details that only the killer would have known. There was an element of doubt however, as to De Salvo's guilt based on a forensic psychiatric report from the state hospital stating that De Salvo couldn't be "The Strangler" because "he didn't hate his mother enough." The Massachusetts Attorney General decided that De Salvo should undergo polygraph testing. Just minutes before the test was to be given, De Salvo slit his wrists. In my opinion, it was an obvious attempt to avoid the test. He knew the test would confirm that he was "The Boston Strangler" and the validity of the confession that he had made to Attorney Bailey. To my knowledge, he never again agreed to take a polygraph test.

The Boston Police had their eyes on De Salvo for some time prior to Attorney Bailey getting De Salvo's confession. They believed he could be "The Boston Strangler" based on his arrest record and aberrant sexual behavior. Their suspicions were undermined by the psychiatric report. They didn't even doubt that report until Attorney Bailey got his confession. As I think back on this case, it's amazing to me how that one premise, that he "didn't hate his mother enough" would carry more weight than all of De Salvo's past behavior.

You have to work on a lot of cases and endure bitter lessons to learn all the potential pitfalls in criminal investigation. Sometimes, no matter how much experience you have, a case will just defy human analysis.

THE MIRANDA WARNING

This topic has caused me more consternation than any other subject discussed in this book. Over the years, I've had conflicting thoughts about the Fifth Amendment to the Constitution and The Miranda Ruling. I've been unable to have a fixed belief about the general goodness or badness of either one. Although I have been interrogating people for over half a century, I can't fix in my mind an ideal legal format for criminal interrogation.

The problem for me is, how do you create a format that protects individual rights but allows sufficient latitude for the police to determine truth? Trying to create that balance is a problem so perplexing that it appears to defy human ingenuity. The technicians of the law have attempted to solve this problem by Supreme Court rulings that have, in essence, constitutionalized police work. The Supreme Court decisions represent a continuing trend to tighten the reins on the police. It's hard to argue against an effort to prevent injustices, but the result may be a criminal justice system that cannot guarantee the constitutional right to domestic tranquility.

The framework and the genesis for every Supreme Court decision regarding criminal interrogation has been the Fifth Amendment to the Constitution. The concept of the Fifth Amendment to the Constitution undoubtedly stemmed from the general reputation of the English Court of Start Chamber, an inquisitorial court that forced people to testify about their religious beliefs. Eventually, the English Parliament abolished the English Court of Start Chamber, but the memory of that abhorrent court was carried over to America, and was the basis for the Fifth Amendment, which states, "No person shall be compelled in any criminal case, to be a witness against himself, or to be deprived of life, liberty or property without due process of the law."

The Fifth Amendment established a definite procedure for questioning in courts of law, but not in the police station. For over 100 years, the court closed their eyes to the conduct of the police when they questioned criminal suspects. The Wickersham Report of the 1930s, a report emanating from a presidential commission, made the court in this country aware that they had to do something about police abuses in criminal interrogation. That report revealed that abusive police conduct was a nationwide problem. It also revealed that the courts had to do something because the police, on their own, were not going to do anything to rectify the problem. Thus began the constitutionalization of police work in America. The creation of laws pertaining to arrest, search and seizure, were more easily stated than creating guidelines for police interrogation. It is a subject so perplexing in nature that it defies the creation of definitive standards. Some people have suggested that to eliminate the problem, we should outlaw all police interrogation. That proposal, in my opinion, is tantamount to suggesting that we outlaw the pursuit of truth.

The absolute truth is contained only in the mind of the perpetrator. He alone can reveal the motive and the precise details of the crime. He alone can reveal hidden bodies, weapons and stolen items. Without a confession, too many aspects of the crime are left unresolved. The court in *Trilling vs. United States*, voiced its recognition of a necessity for police interrogation. "The usual, most useful, most efficient and most effective method of investigation is by questioning people. It is all very well to say that the police should investigate by microscopic examination of stains and dust. Sometimes they can. But, of all the human facilities for ascertaining the facts, asking questions is the usual one and has always been. The courts use that method."

Prior to the Miranda Supreme Court ruling of 1966, the courts handed down a myriad of decisions primarily concerning the voluntariness of a confession. Succinctly stated, what the courts wanted was a confession given of a person's own free will, and obtained without physical or psychological abuse or promises. To some self-interested groups, these guidelines weren't sufficient. They wanted all police interrogation to be outlawed, or no interrogation was to be conducted unless the suspect's attorney was present. In truth, the fight for Miranda Supreme Court ruling was a compromise. It left intact the right of the police to interrogate, but provided additional safeguards to protect the suspect. The prominent safeguards are the right to remain silent, the right to have an attorney present at the time of the interrogation, and the right to have an attorney appointed for the suspect before any interrogation took place. In retrospect, the Miranda Ruling leaves unresolved three important questions, "Was it needed?," "Has it been beneficial to society?," and "Has it been detrimental to police work?"

If I were a member of a debate team trying to answer these questions, I could argue for either the affirmative side or the negative side with equal enthusiasm. That's the reason this topic is so exasperating to me. In response to the first question, I have to concede that the Fifth Amendment and Miranda Ruling are noble concepts reflecting the values of a highly civilized society. However, it is also my opinion, that you can follow a principle to your death knell. It's difficult to argue against any effort to prevent injustices, but the result may be a criminal justice system that cannot guarantee the constitutional right to domestic tranquility.

The Supreme Court recently upheld the Miranda Ruling stating that, "The Miranda Warning has become ingrained in the American culture" despite the argument from those who opposed it that in reality the Warning acerbates the crime problem. Any suggestion that the Fifth Amendment or the Miranda Warning be modified is immediately met with a charge of blasphemy. From a philosophical standpoint, I appreciate the nobility of these concepts, but, from a practical standpoint, they make police work more difficult. Both concepts are safe harbors for those who choose to withhold the truth.

It seems to me, that, in this point and time, wherein our society has reached a high degree of sophistication, we should be capable of creating a criminal justice system that doesn't give such an illogical edge to the criminal. The overwhelming injustice in this country is the millions of people victimized by criminals because of the restrictions placed on the police in their effort to prove guilt. One day, we're going to have to ask ourselves, how much crime should we endure to continue to satisfy the belief by some self-interest groups that the police are the real enemy.

In my career, I worked on three cases where four people were convicted of first-degree murder, and their convictions were based on false confessions. Those who falsely confessed were Joe Shea, Mary K. Hampton, Freddie Pitts, and Wilbert Lee. I played a role in helping free all four individuals from prison. In the *Pitts-Lee* case, I obtained a confession from Curtis Adams, who actually committed the murders for which Pitts and Lee were convicted.

I know from personal experience that false confessions do occur.

They are caused by prolonged and unchecked interrogations. Because of human nature, and despite the safeguards, false confessions will continue to occur. In my opinion, the occasional false confession doesn't justify the accusation that the police are the enemy. The problem of false confessions is minuscule compared to the amount of people convicted of crimes because of wrong identifications. This is particularly true in armed robbery cases. I wonder if those who believe that all police interrogation should be eliminated, would also suggest that witness identification be eliminated as evidence.

I believe that there should be legal guidelines for police interrogation. They should be realistic and practical in nature. What concerns me the most is the illogicalness of the current legal guidelines. Through parental training, school education, and religious influence, we place great emphasis on the moral responsibility of telling the truth. In comparison, the primary defense of our criminal justice system is the right to withhold the truth.

I have lived long enough to have 15 years of interrogational experience prior to the Miranda ruling, and 35 years of experience in issuing the Miranda Warning. The statisticians have offered conflicting results regarding the impact of the Miranda Warning. The simple truth is that, in my career, I obtained more confessions prior to the Miranda ruling. Suspects who waive their right to be silent sign the Miranda Warning for three reasons: They are innocent, they don't want to appear guilty, or they think they can lie successfully. What the interrogators lost with the Miranda Warning were a percentage of suspects who potentially would confess but declined to do so after being advised that they had a legal [converted in their mind to *moral*] right to remain silent. It's been my experience that the Miranda Warning abates guilt feelings in suspects. The warning destroys, with those who refuse to waive their rights, the powerful interrogational argument that the suspect has a moral obligation to tell the truth.

The major impact of the Miranda Warning is the fact that it became a crutch for the lazy police officer. That is the irony of the Miranda Warning. Many police officers detest interrogation, and are quick to abort the process. They believe that failure to get a confession reflects on their proficiency. The Miranda Warning became an out for those investigators not inclined to persevere. For all of the stated reasons, I don't believe the Miranda Warning has been beneficial to this society, and has definitely been detrimental to police work. It is, however, the *law of the land*, and should be obeyed in its broadest terms.

Chapter II

NONACCUSATORY INTERROGATION

After the interrogator has listened to a brief synopsis of the suspect's story, he should have some idea of the suspect's defense, whether it's based on innocence or guilt. To reach a more definitive conclusion as to innocence or guilt, in-depth questioning is required. The questioning should be done in a nonaccusatory manner so as not to alienate either an innocent or guilty person. The interrogator's questioning should reflect a sincere effort to understand what occurred.

Nonaccusatory interrogation is not *cross-examination*, which is done to discredit someone in a court of law. That approach creates an acrimonious relationship between the suspect and the interrogator and undermines the goal of obtaining a confession. Keep in mind that the whole purpose of nonaccusatory interrogation is to facilitate the decision to make a transition to accusatory interrogation. This decision is more difficult when the evidence in the case is just circumstantial.

Before I start questioning a suspect regarding the case, I like to get some idea of the nature of the person I'm speaking to. That requires taking biographical data and general background information. There are two sayings which I believe are applicable, "When you know a man's past, you know his future," and "A man's character is his fate." Taking biographical data gives the impression that the interview is going to be thorough and creates what I call "benevolent dominance." The suspect realizes that a structured format is going to be used. That undermines the confidence of the guilty, but is reassuring to the innocent. While taking biographical data you see for the first time, the degree of cooperation or defensiveness you're going to get from the suspect. If he is defensive on the less threatening questions you can be sure that attitude will prevail throughout the interview. Taking biographical data invites the suspect to lie and may provide a wedge to be used later in accusatory interrogation.

Suspects lie about their real name, arrest record, job history, service record, psychiatric treatment, drug and alcohol abuse and prior accusations of wrongdoing. If they lie about their general background that sets up the accusatory interrogation argument, "If you lied about that, you'll lie about anything." Discussing the suspect's arrest record affords the best opportunity to assess what you are up against. "Did he plead guilty to prior offenses?," "Did he confess or did he take the attitude that everyone in the world is wrong but him?" Job history gives you the same insights.

In larceny cases, it's extremely helpful to find out if the suspect is the common denominator in past cases and in the current one. To do this you have to bluff in the following way: "Before I asked you to come to my office we did a background check and credit check on you. So before you answer these questions I want you to think very carefully. Have you ever been fired under suspicion of theft or accused of stealing on a job? Now think carefully before you answer those questions." Make sure you ask the questions as though you already know the answers. If the bluff works and the answer is affirmative, follow-up by saying, "OK. I already know about the past accusation against you but I want to test your truthfulness by hearing your side of the story." If the past wrongdoing is similar in nature to the one under investigation, odds are that you have the right person and you can use the past thefts as a wedge to attempt to get a confession on the current case.

The thrust of the interview in larceny cases is to bluff the suspect into revealing a source of income he can't explain. Use the same technique previously explained. "Again, I want you to think carefully before you answer this question. In the past three months, what is the most expensive thing you have purchased, and the biggest bill you have paid? Be careful, don't lie to this question." When the suspect tells you what he bought or what bill he paid off, if it's significant in nature, you must follow up as to where he got the money. This is where he will lie. The threat of verifying the source of money is a good wedge toward getting a confession.

In fraud and arson cases, obtaining a detailed financial picture of the suspect's indebtedness will indicate possible motive. Any resistance on his part to reveal indebtedness is often an indication of guilt especially if the suspect says, "I think those questions are personal." It has been my experience that innocent people are generally up front in responding to all questions concerning biographical data and general background.

In bank cases, tellers who steal will directly or indirectly reveal that there are personal problems at home. Often, indebtedness, sickness or marital problems are the motives for thefts committed by bank tellers. That information can be used in the accusatory interrogation by pointing out to the suspect, "I've talked to you long enough to know that you are basically a good person but I believe that your personal problems got you to the point where you were desperate and you didn't care anymore. I think you stole the money because of personal problems not because of bad character." I've used this argument hundreds of times with bank tellers and found it to be most effective.

Problems in the military service are sometimes a precursor of wrong behavior in civilian life. When a suspect hesitates or is reluctant to answer questions regarding his service record that means his credibility is suspect. You can really be conned if you fail to ask questions about the suspect's personal habits, particularly their use of alcohol, prescription and illegal drugs. Alcoholics and drug addicts are masters of disassociation. Heavy cocaine-users have mashed potato brains and other than psychopaths are the most prolific liars. The continuing practice of self-deception in people with substance abuse problems makes them very convincing liars.

While taking the background information, I try to make an assessment as to the person's social intelligence, or what policemen call "street smarts." Some people have a Ph.D. in duping others. In fact, they get a sense of joy in doing so and a feeling of power. With this type of suspect, you have less chance of getting a confession, but at least you're not fooled. When the interrogator completes the general background and biographical data, he should have some insight as to whether or not this particular suspect has a propensity to commit the act in question. In this respect, one of the most fruitful areas to cover is whether or not the suspect has ever visited a psychologist or psychiatrist or undergone any psychiatric therapy for a significant period of time. You should also determine whether he has ever been institutionalized for a mental condition.

I once accused a man of murder when there was no evidence that a murder had been committed. According to the police, the suspect had an airtight alibi for the period of time during which his employer mysteriously disappeared. However, the family of the employer was suspicious of the recently fired employee and offered him money to take a polygraph test. He readily agreed to do so. During the pretest interview, I found out that the ex-employee had once turned himself in at a hospital because he had "weird feelings about committing violence." This had occurred in another state years before the disappearance of his employer. The minute I learned this, I started looking at the suspect with a "fish eye." I was convinced even before the test that this employee had killed his boss. He definitely had the propensity to do so and the test results confirmed my suspicions.

I told the police and the family members that the employee had in fact killed his employer. My opinion caused controversy, particularly after it was publicized. I really stuck my neck out and the case could have been a total embarrassment to me; let alone the anguish I brought to the family members by telling them that their loved one was dead. Several days after the test the employer's body was found in a storm sewer behind his warehouse along with evidence incriminating the man I had tested. The police went to his house to apprehend him and found out he had left town right after the polygraph test. The police located him in Virginia and he confessed to killing his boss. I didn't get the confession in this particular case, but it was one of the most satisfying ones I have worked on. I am convinced that a thorough pretest interview gave me the insight to reach the conclusion that this man was a murderer and that opinion was later bolstered by the polygraph test results. It later turned out that all of the witnesses who had given the man the so-called airtight alibi were wrong.

Each category you cover in taking the biographical data and general background is a potential gold mine of arguments to be used in the accusatory phase of the interrogation. But there is another reason to be thorough in taking the background information. Defense attorneys can embarrass you in a courtroom during cross-examination by revealing information about a defendant you didn't know at the time you took the confession. Such information includes the subject's educational level, history of psychiatric treatment, epilepsy and the influence of drugs and alcohol. You want to be in a position to testify that you knew all of the pertinent information that could have a bearing on the voluntariness of the confession so that your thoroughness lends credibility to your testimony.

Sometimes you will hear a person say, "He couldn't have done it, he has no motive." In many cases motive is not obvious. The motive may stem from the intricacies of the suspect's mind. Even an imagined grievance may be sufficient motive to commit the act. Over the years, I've learned that "something never comes from nothing;" there's always a catalyst. Just because the motive isn't obvious doesn't mean there isn't one. The interrogator may not have dug deep enough to uncover it.

After completing the background and biographical data, you should begin to question the suspect regarding the case. The literature is devoid of information on how to question. Oddly enough, I don't even know of a law school that teaches the art of cross-examination. Over the years I have developed a format for questioning that I think will be of benefit to you.

Attitude

To be successful you have to know the variables that affect questioning. The first and most important is the interrogator's attitude and demeanor. Some interrogators are not assertive enough or do not ask sufficient questions. They sit there listening to the suspect like a human tape recorder. A good interrogator with imagination creates theories in his mind, which are then used as a format to suggest which questions he should ask. Some interrogators are reluctant to create an acrimonious environment so they don't ask the hard questions. Other interrogators identify with the suspect and want to believe him. This creates a mindset of, "There but for the grace of God, go I." The interrogator who has prejudged the suspect's guilt will not ask sufficient questions because he believes it is a waste of time.

Amount to Evaluate

The second factor influencing questioning is how much information you have to evaluate. If the suspect has to describe his behavior over a period of time then he is more susceptible to penetrating questions. If he keeps his story tight as most good liars do, then you will have a more difficult task. The more details a suspect has to relate the better your chance of a definitive evaluation of what the suspect has to say.

Lead Time

The third factor influencing questioning is how much time the suspect had to prepare his lies. Given enough time, suspects will create a story that they think is convincing. They will attempt to fill in the holes in their story, and offer some explanation for the evidence and witness testimony against them. Contrary to what a lot of people think, they never get to the point where they believe the story themselves but they do learn to simulate innocence. They are convinced the story sounds good and gain confidence, which diminishes the signs of their guilt. Adding to their persuasiveness is the fact that in time, natural defense mechanisms enter the picture allowing guilty suspects to justify and rationalize the act committed. For these people guilt is projected outwardly and they make themselves the victim rather than the perpetrator. It pays to question someone early on before they are thoroughly entrenched in denial.

The primary purpose of questioning is to determine that the transition to accusatory interrogation should be made. To make that decision, astute questioning should reveal the following:

1. Is the suspect too defensive?
2. Is the suspect unnecessarily hostile?
3. Is the suspect non-responsive to the questions?
4. Is the suspect overly evasive in his replies?
5. Are the suspect's replies nonsensical in nature?
6. Is there too much hesitation in the suspect's answers?
7. Does his body language reveal a lack of confidence in his story?

If there is one secret to good questioning, it is the tactic of constantly pushing the suspect to be more explicit in his answers. This tactic is unnerving to the liar because he is relying on made-up answers, not memory recall. The innocent can answer any question and their answers are limited only by faulty memory. The guilty on the other hand have a level of defense that can be penetrated and shattered by questions they never anticipated.

Thorough questioning reveals whether the suspect is relying on memory or crafted response. A word of caution, some people with a well-prepared story can look good under questioning for more than an hour when suddenly the interrogator asks one question that they did not anticipate and their whole demeanor changes. At that moment, they realize that the interrogator sees a hole in their story they can't reconcile and they lose confidence. With that single question they start showing signs of guilt that were not previously evident. Finding a hole in their story can save you from being duped by a suspect who has crafted a clever story.

In the following pages, I've set forth some suggested rules for questioning. I think they have application in any type of case.

Chapter III

QUESTIONING

Rule One: Always Question Chronologically

Questioning innocent people chronologically helps them recall a sequence of events particularly if you start by asking them what they were doing several hours prior to the time period in question. Covering their behavior several hours prior to the crime gets them thinking chronologically and can even enhance memory recall. Getting a detailed description of their behavior prior to, during, and after the crime relaxes the innocent suspect because your thoroughness gives him confidence that you're going to establish the truth.

With the guilty suspect, it is unnerving. He begins to see a thoroughness that he never anticipated. The interrogator's thoroughness creates a dominance, which then enhances the manifestations of guilt. Psychopaths and those with a rehearsed story do not like to be questioned; they like to do the talking to maintain a dominant position. When you run into this problem simply tell the suspect, "I listened to you. Now I want you to follow my format." Chronological questioning forces the guilty suspect to create lies to unexpected questions in contrast to the innocent suspect who is simply recalling the truth. Without a basis in factual memory, the guilty have difficulty telling the same story twice. Chronological questioning brings out more details and the guilty suspect can't keep track of what he's fabricated. The innocent does not have this problem, as the truth never varies.

Chronological questioning allows you to judge what the guilty emphasize and what they gloss over. The guilty always emphasize safe areas and avoid a detailed description of their behavior at the time of the crime. In comparison, the innocent offers vivid and descriptive details because they are bolstered by their confidence in the truth as they get to the juicy part of the story.

Rule Two: The First Category of Questions Pertaining to the Crime Should Be to Determine the Catalyst

State of Mind

Your first questions of the suspect should be designed to determine state of mind. Find out if anything happened preceding the crime that could have prompted him to commit the act.

I worked on a case where an employee of a major airport was accused of deliberately driving his vehicle into several young people who were walking along the side of the road. The incident happened at night. Some of them were killed. It was difficult for me to conceive that anyone would want to knock down pedestrians like bowling pins.

Using chronological questioning I started with the time the employee got out of bed and I went through his entire day. I was not coming up with anything that would have put him into an unusually bad mood until I started asking him about where he went after work. It turned out that he had gone to his girlfriend's house and they had a violent argument. He left the house angry at the world. As he was driving along he saw the young people and became incensed that they were blocking half of the road. He told me that he had just intended to scare them but inadvertently lost control causing their deaths. This is a tragic example of the cause of most crimes, Loss of self-control. Ask questions to determine if anything could have prompted the suspect to experience a loss of self-control. Look for the presence of drug or substance abuse, which are the enemies of self-control.

Sometimes personal problems build to a crescendo so that inhibitions cease to function and the person commits a crime that he wouldn't have under normal circumstances. The motive for the crime may be the build-up of frustration over a long period of time. When something triggers the person, he releases the pent-up frustration in a murderous impulse or commits an act which defies his general nature and reputation. Not achieving one's goals, losing respect, and rejection are all underlying factors in the commission of crimes. Ferret out any personal problems that could create a mood or attitude that would prompt the person to commit the crime.

Talking about life in general, an astute interrogator can get the suspect to indirectly reveal his state of mind. "Something never comes from nothing." Every overt act has an antecedent condition. The thrust of the questioning under Rule Two is to determine if the suspect had any reason to commit the crime.

Changes in Routine

While questioning under Rule Two, determine if the suspect changed his normal routine. A change in routine could have been done deliberately to set up an alibi, direct suspicion toward another person, or "open the crime up to the world." If the suspect admits that he was in the area of the crime, but denies guilt, the interrogator should get a detailed description as to why he was in the area.

Mistakes

Someone not predisposed to commit an act may do so because of someone else's mistake or a change in circumstances. In commercial cases, such as bank thefts, this happens because someone inadvertently leaves money unattended which gives another employee the opportunity to steal. He thinks, "No one will suspect *me*."

Oddly enough, the catalyst, which is someone else's mistake also becomes the justification for the act. I've had many guilty people tell me, "The money shouldn't have been left out."

Rule Three: Ask Questions to Differentiate Between Memory Recall and Fantasy

Level of Detail

When truthful people tell a story, faulty memory is their only limitation. When guilty people tell a story, that story is limited by their imagination. Simply put, when you question someone you have to ask yourself, "Is he relating what occurred as best as he can or is he making it up as he hears the questions?" You can't run out of the truth, but you can run out of imagination. Constantly forcing the suspect to be more explicit is the best way to ascertain if you're dealing with memory recall or fantasy.

Every guilty person has a level of defense. That defense has been created in preparation for potential questions. The interrogator has to think of questions the guilty person never anticipated. As the guilty person is forced to keep thinking up new aspects of his story you will begin to see manifestations of guilt such as nonsensical replies or hesitation as he tries to think of a plausible answer. As previously indicated, liars keep their stories tight with few details to reduce the burden of creativity.

Incidental Details

I conducted the first polygraph test in the Watergate Investigation. I tested the young man who worked in a Miami photography studio who developed the film taken by the Watergate burglars. The photographs depicted close-ups of Democratic Party stationery. The young man, who had read about the Watergate burglary in the newspaper went to several different law enforcement agencies and told them that he thought he had developed film for the Watergate burglars. They disbelieved him and thought he was a publicity-seeker. Exasperated, he finally went to the office of the State attorney, who sent him to me.

When he arrived in my office, he was a nervous wreck because nobody would believe him. As he told his story, he provided so many details regarding what was in the photographs that I couldn't understand why he was previously disbelieved. I was convinced he was telling the truth even before I administered the polygraph test. After the test, I told the State Attorney's office that the young man was telling the truth. The burglars' attorney went on national television and denied that his clients had ever been in the photography studio. He stated that my polygraph test results were wrong. Several days later a Cuban employee confirmed that the burglars had been in the shop and were supposed to have given him the film but he was busy with other customers at the time. The burglars later admitted that they had brought the film into the photography studio.

This case highlights my contention that a description of incidental details confirms the validity of a story. The young man had told me that the Cuban employee was extremely nervous while the burglars were in the store. It was later confirmed that the Cuban employee conspired with the burglars in advance to develop the film.

Only innocent people provide incidental details that can be verified. In real life, things do not happen in a vacuum. Generally, there are simultaneous events that occur even at a crime scene, such as a man walking a dog, a passing ambulance with its siren blaring, or a man changing a tire alongside the road. Verifying the incidental detail that emanates from memory can confirm the truthfulness of the entire story.

Nervous Guilty vs. Nervous Innocent

As previously indicated, fear contaminates memory. The interrogator has to differentiate between the "nervous innocent" and the "nervous guilty." One difference is that the guilty use convenient and selective memory by not responding to even the most innocuous questions because to do so would unmask the "faulty memory" defense. Another difference is that the guilty do not manifest, in body language or demeanor, the frustration of not being able to remember. That frustration is readily seen in the innocent.

A good sign that someone is lying is that he tells you a detail that should automatically suggest another detail, but omits the second detail. He may later claim that he forgot about the second detail, but if a person remembers "A" he should remember "B." Failure to do so is a good indicator that he lied about detail "A."

Rule Four: Ask Verification Questions

When all you have is the suspect's word, you should try to get some form of verification. You can do this by asking:
1. "Who knows this besides you?"
2. "Who witnessed the act?"
3. "Who shared the same experience?"
4. "Who was the first person you told about what occurred?"

Failure to Relate

If the storyteller is unable to provide verification through another witness, then the most important question is, "Whom did you first talk to about this?" Failure to discuss the incident with a wife, close relative or friend raises doubts as to the validity of the story. People are recognition junkies. They love to be in the limelight when relating an experience. Failure to relate the experience is a good indication of guilt or the crafting of a false story.

I've already mentioned the case of the fired employee who killed his boss as an example of the importance of a thorough pretest interview. That case also provided me with a classic example of "failure to relate. . . ." During the pretest interview I asked him, "Did you talk to your wife about the disappearance of your ex-boss and the fact that you are a suspect in his disappearance?" He said, "We don't discuss such things at the dinner table."

Feelings

Innocent people describe feelings; the guilty generally do not. If the information is not volunteered, then, indirectly, without tipping your hand, this has to be discussed. Don't let the guilty suspect know that you're suspicious because he hasn't mentioned feelings. When innocent people tell a story they relive the emotions. Their facial expressions match their words. Lacking any other verification, a vivid description is a good indicator of truthfulness. The whole essence of this verification technique is that the feelings were voluntarily expressed and didn't come about in response to a direct question.

Tangible Verification

If the storyteller cannot provide human verification you have to determine if he can provide any other type of verification such as work records, journal entries, receipts, etc. One of the best tests for verification is the question, "Are you willing to take a lie detector test?" There are very few legitimate excuses for refusing to take a polygraph test. It should be noted that many people who say they are willing to take a test will back out later.

Consistency

If the suspect has related his story to other investigators, the interrogator should ask questions to determine the consistency of the story. Any major differences that cannot be reconciled are generally an indicator that the story has been fabricated.

I worked on a case where someone was stealing large amounts of cash from a Miami hospital emergency room. The money accrued from patients who had paid for their emergency room services in cash.

To resolve the problem, the personnel resource officer asked several employees to submit to polygraph examinations. One employee, to divert suspicion from himself, mentioned to the resource officer that he had found a threatening note on the windshield of his car. The resource officer told me about the note, but when the suspect came to my office, he never mentioned it. From experience, I knew that omission was a significant inconsistency and indicated probable guilt in the theft of the cash. After the test, the suspect confessed to the thefts.

Rule Five: Ask Questions That Test the Logic of the Story

Why?

An interrogator should always ask himself the question, "Is this what a normal human being would have done in a similar situation?" This is not an absolute guideline, but most of the time anything in the story that deviates from what the average person would have done is a lie. An interrogator should always ask why a person did something in each sequence of events. Suspects find it much more difficult to lie about why they did something than about what they did. A guilty suspect creates a story expecting to be asked questions about *what* he did, not *why* he did it. The "Why?" questions prompt better signs of lying.

One of my favorite techniques is to question the subject regarding alternative options. When you question a person about why he did a particular thing rather than something else, watch to see how vigorously he defends what he did when it is obvious that another course of action would have been better. The innocent will generally say, "Yeah, I guess that was stupid. I should have done something else." By comparison, the guilty person will have to defend his activity because he's trapped in a lie about what he did. You can apply further pressure to reveal signs of lying by asking the subject, "You did 'A' rather than 'B,' why did you do anything at all?"

Omissions

In testing the logic of a story, sometimes what a person doesn't say is more important than what he does say. If a logical thought is not expressed, it should raise suspicion in the interrogator's mind. For example, if only one other person besides the suspect could have stolen the money, and the suspect says he has no suspicions about that person, that undermines his contention of innocence. Logic would dictate that if he did not steal the money, he would have to think the other person did. An innocent person would raise the suspicion even if reluctant to cast aspersions.

In the interrogation of the ex-employee who murdered his boss, I asked what he thought might have happened to his employer. He gave several alternative explanations for his disappearance but never once mentioned the possibility of death. That exclusion was highly significant in my mind. Guilty people leave out of speculation what they know actually occurred.

Hole in the Story

If a story has a major hole, it cannot be considered logical. Often a guilty suspect will craft a very persuasive story but it will have one hole in it that he cannot reconcile. An inexperienced interrogator may overlook this hole because the rest of the story is so convincing. That is a fatal mistake. Even in an innocent person's story, you can't always make all the pieces of the puzzle fit because of faulty memory, coincidence or chance. But a hole that can't be explained by one of these factors is generally caused by a lie. When evaluating the likelihood of deception, the hole in the story outweighs the rest of the story, no matter how persuasive.

A word of caution, do not fill in the hole for the suspect. Do not say, "Now is it possible that. . . ?" offering a logical explanation for the hole. The guilty suspect will say to himself, "That's good. I wish I had thought of that." He will then reply to the interrogator, "Yeah, that's probably what happened." Do not help the suspect make his story better. The hole in the suspect's story is a wedge to be used in accusatory interrogation. Don't destroy the wedge by filling in the hole for him.

Rule Six: Ask Questions That Reveal the Use of the Defense Mechanisms of Projection And Disassociation

If I were limited to the use of only one question to render an opinion as to the guilt or innocence of a suspect, the question would be, "What is your theory about this crime?" Innocent people are by nature "armchair detectives." They love the theorizing stage of inter-rogation because it gives them an opportunity to demonstrate how smart they are. Guilty people on the other hand are unnerved by that question because it forces them to talk about something they are try-ing to avoid or suppress. A lack of theorizing shows defensiveness or that they have no need to theorize because they already know the answer. Reluctance to theorize also indicates a lack of desire to satis-fy normal curiosity. Innocent people show an interest in trying to fig-ure out what happened. Guilty people show little or no interest.

When you ask questions pertaining to theories or suspicions and you get evasive answers, that clearly indicates that the defense mech-anism of disassociation is operative. To test for the defense mechanism of projection ask the following questions:

1. "Why is the accuser saying this about you?"
2. "Do you think the accuser made up this story?"
3. "Do you think the witness is lying?"
4. "Do you think this is a real theft or a clerical error?"

Any lack of objectivity or honest acknowledgement of a possibility is a definite sign that the defense mechanism of projection is being used.

Rule Seven: When You Have Nothing to Evaluate You Have to Force an Evaluation

When you question a suspect about a crime he will either connect or disconnect to the act in question. If he connects he will confess to the crime or he will lie his way out of it by offering a plausible expla-nation for why he was there and what he was doing. An innocent per-son may connect to the crime, but profess to be a victim of circum-stance. With both the innocent and the guilty who admit connection, you have something to evaluate. They have to explain why they were there and what they did.

The difficult cases are those where both the innocent and the guilty disconnect, leaving you no substantive story to evaluate. They will both utter the same remark, "I wasn't there." I don't know anything about it." Then you are left with only one thing, the suspect's alibi. Thorough questioning about the alibi is a good substitute when you have no story to evaluate.

Innocent people demonstrate an air of confidence when relating their alibi. They look and sound truthful. The guilty on the other hand, appear evasive discussing their alibi and fail to verify it with independent witnesses or documentation. There is one exception to this and that is when the guilty person has deliberately set up an alibi to exclude himself from the crime. This suspect will go overboard to verify the alibi revealing that he anticipated having to prove his whereabouts at the time of the crime. You see this premeditated alibi-overkill particularly in arson cases. In a plan to defraud the insurance company, the suspect makes arrangements for his home to be set on fire. He then leaves town and goes to great pains to document his whereabouts. This reveals his guilt.

If a guilty suspect disconnects from a crime, he does so both physically and mentally. This affords the interrogator the opportunity for another evaluation. See how comfortable the suspect is just talking about the crime in general. The innocent will demonstrate both empathy and sympathy with such remarks as, "Isn't it terrible, I can't believe it happened." The guilty further their detachment by a dispassionate attitude toward the crime.

Rule Eight: Ask Questions to Determine Post-Act Behavior

When a person commits a crime, from that moment on he is in a posture of self-defense. Suspects will generally manifest signs of guilt or wrongdoing through a change in behavior. I have seen them attempt suicide, check into a hospital with a sudden illness, leave town, quit a job, get drunk or contact an attorney before even being accused. In several instances, I've worked on a case where the person was so angry with himself for committing the crime that he engaged in bizarre behavior or life-threatening acts like reckless driving or drowning. Questions concerning post-act behavior catch a suspect off guard because they generally don't anticipate being asked about their behavior after the crime.

Any change in the suspect's routine should be considered significant because it may be prompted by the commission of the crime. Many years ago, I worked on a case where $1,400 was stolen from a safe in a real estate office. The first person I tested was a little old lady who told me the tests were a waste of time, because she knew who had stolen the money. I asked her, "How do you know that?" She replied,

"Because for ten years, Harry has always gone to lunch at exactly 12:00 o'clock. On the day the money was stolen he went to lunch at 11:45. Only nervousness could make him change his routine." That little old lady was right. Harry did steal the $1,400. He hid the money in his car. He left early for lunch to drive home and take the stolen money out of his car.

The perpetrator may do something nice in an attempt to compensate (at least in his mind) for what he did wrong. He will buy flowers for his wife or take his fellow employees out to lunch with the stolen money. When you ask questions concerning post-act behavior, be careful not to let the suspect know that you're looking for any behavior which might have been prompted by the commission of the crime.

Rule Nine: You Can't Think of Every
Question You Should Ask

During the early part of my career, I discovered that many people did not volunteer critical information because I failed to ask them specific questions. My failure provided them with an excuse to deliberately withhold pertinent information. All of these people had decided, "I'm not going to tell him if he doesn't ask me." Now, I do not let them off the hook so easily. I conclude my questioning with an all-encompassing question; "Is there anything you didn't tell me because I didn't ask you the question?" It is amazing how often I receive the response, "Well, there is one thing."

When you have finished your questioning and concluded that the person is lying, you have to make one of the most critical transitions in interrogation: The transition from nonaccusatory to accusatory interrogation.

Chapter IV

HOW PEOPLE LIE

When I finish my questions and I've made the decision to move from nonaccusatory interrogation to accusatory interrogation, that decision, aside from the evidence in the case, is based on the information in this chapter.

Liars have only one strategy in mind, which is to convince the interrogator that they're telling the truth. To do that, they employ certain tactics and make predictable statements. It has been my experience that liars lie the same way. I have categorized the liar statements, remarks and expressions that are familiar to all experienced interrogators.

Statements, Remarks and Expressions

A. Loophole Statements
1. "To the best of my knowledge."
2. "Not that I remember."
3. "Not that I'm aware."
4. "Not that I can think of."

Sometimes an innocent person will utter these remarks because he really can't remember and he doesn't want to mislead the interrogator. But the liar makes these statements to avoid being pinned down. The difference between the two, is the frequency of use. Loophole statements are a tool of the tactic of evasiveness. Loophole statements are actually qualifiers so that the user cannot later be accused of deliberately lying.

B. Over-Sell Expressions
  1. "Honestly"
  2. "To be honest"
  3. "Truthfully"
  4. "Frankly"
  5. "Believe me"
  6. "May I drop dead. . . ."
  7. "I swear to God. . . ."
  8. "May I swear on my mother's grave. . . ."
  9. "May my wife and children burn in hell. . . ."

These expressions are designed to add more weight to what follows them and to make that more believable. Liars find it difficult to respond with a simple "yes" or "no." To appear credible, they always add something.

C. Thinking-Time Statements
  1. "Who me?"
  2. "What was that question?"
  3. "Can you repeat the question?"
  4. "I don't understand the question."
  5. "What did you say?"
  6. "Are you asking me that question?"
  7. "Uh. . . ."
  8. "Why should I have to answer that, that was a long time ago. . . ."
  9. "Do you want me to tell you the truth?"

One of the more obvious signs of lying is that the person hesitates before responding to a direct question. The reason is simple; you have to think before you lie. Thinking-time statements are interjections before the response is made. In that sense they differ from loophole statements, which is the response.

D. Brooklyn Bridge Remarks
  1. "I didn't steal the money, but I feel morally obligated to pay it back."
  2. "I need to know if I did it."

Some remarks are both comical and an insult to your intelligence. They indicate the suspect is at a halfway point between not confessing and confessing. They are made by people who are trying to work up the nerve to confess.

E. Offense Statements
   1. "Why should I lie?"
   2. "Do you want me to tell a lie on myself?"
   3. "Are you accusing me?"
   4. "Are you calling me a liar?"
   5. "Why would I do anything like that?"
   6. "Are you trying to put words in my mouth?"

These statements are made by design to put the interrogator on the defensive. It's the old story of the best defense is a good offense. In making these statements, the suspect is trying to take control of the interview. If the interrogator doesn't answer these questions in a forceful manner he's in trouble. The interrogator can regain dominance by telling the suspect precisely why the suspect asked the question. Point out to the suspect that he asked the question as an evasive tactic and to avoid the responsibility of giving a direct answer to the question.

Tactics

Tactics in lying emanate from defense mechanisms. I believe that defense mechanisms are instinctive and are a necessary ingredient in the evolutionary process. Defense mechanisms are a vehicle for homeostasis in a life victimized by trauma or intolerable thought processes. They are a means of avoiding acceptance of one's wrong-doing. The defense mechanisms that you encounter most frequently in any interrogation session are projection, disassociation, rationalization, and identification.

Almost all of the tactics employed by liars are encompassed by these four defense mechanisms. In our context, I like the following working definitions:

- Projection: Displacement of blame outside oneself, to another or to society in general.
- Disassociation: A "thinking-away" process, a compartmentalizing of the mind to exclude guilty thoughts. Both actions are a conscious effort to enhance denial.
- Rationalization: Giving "nice" reasons rather than real reasons, to save face. It's been my experience that people justify an act at the time it's committed or that they seek justification later to make the act tolerable.
- Identification: Attributing moral characteristics to themselves that would preclude them from committing any wrongdoing.

DEFENSE MECHANISMS AND THEIR TACTICS

In the following pages, I'm going to give examples of liar tactics that emanate from the four different defense mechanisms. It should be noted that suspects will sometimes change defense mechanisms as the interrogation process continues. There may be some minor overlapping, but the particular defense mechanism employed is generally identifiable in one of four categories.

Identification

This particular defense mechanism always brings to mind the saying, "Every professed virtue hides a secret vice." The suspect who uses this particular defense mechanism argues a generalized character of goodness rather than a specific innocence. The suspect attempts to give the impression that he is of such good character that he couldn't have possibly committed the act in question. His good character automatically excludes him from suspicion. At least that's the image he's trying to create. The suspect is more comfortable arguing a general goodness than discussing the crime because then he would have to lie.

As an interrogator you sometimes get the impression that when a suspect employs the defense mechanism of identification, he's not only lying to convince you of his goodness, but also himself. You get the impression he's trying too hard to sell himself. His premise is, if they're going to accuse me of lying, let them accuse a saint. This attitude helps him justify his act and minimize the stigma of guilt. Sometimes the defense mechanism of identification is more specific in nature as when the suspect attributes to himself a professed personality characteristic that in his mind excludes him or puts him above suspicion. Human beings are a smorgasbord of personality traits but a good trait does not preclude the potential to commit wrongdoing. In interrogation, the professed good trait can become a barrier to getting a confession because the suspect doesn't want to sacrifice the image of himself he has created with the interrogator by confessing.

I once tested a police lieutenant accused of molesting a child in one of our national parks. He argued that he couldn't have committed the act because he was known for being "good with children." He described how he helped build the police Benevolent Association Children's Park and collected donations to sustain it. All of that was true, but he was also a child molester. His professed virtues became such a strong barrier that I was unable to obtain a confession. Years later, he was arrested for a similar offense.

Sometimes a botched crime is an embarrassment to the perpetrator. It reflects on his intelligence and professed skills. He will then argue that a man of his experience would never have committed the crime in such a haphazard manner. That contention has some basis in truth but the reality is that in this instance he just did a poor job. He is so angry about making a mess of things that he tries to save himself the embarrassment. These suspects create an image of expertise in such activities as marksmanship, martial arts, safe-cracking, burglary, etc. They identify with a level of expertise that in their mind excludes them from the crime in question.

Suspects using the defense mechanism of identification are sometimes obsequious in nature. They try to convey an image of being inoffensive and nice. This demeanor is contrived and is done in an effort to ingratiate themselves with the interrogator. They are saying in effect, "See how nice I am? How could you ever think that I'm guilty?" This oversolicitous and friendly demeanor is not realistic in view of the seriousness of the situation and accusations against them.

The suspect who employs the defense mechanism of identification is always an image-maker. He has a habit of talking in the third person and making himself a witness on his own behalf. For example, when asked "Have you ever stolen anything from the warehouse?" his response would be, "Mr. Holmes, people will tell you that Harry Brown is an honest man. Besides that, everybody who works in the warehouse is honest." The suspect was nonresponsive to the question and the defense mechanism employed is obvious.

Guilty people try to further their image of niceness by refusing to suggest the name of anyone else who could have committed the crime. They assume a holier-than-thou attitude claiming that it wouldn't be fair for them to accuse anyone unless they had actually seen them commit the act. Overstated references to religious beliefs are sometimes another indication that this defense mechanism is being used.

Sometimes this defense mechanism manifests itself as an exclusion due to position. The suspect is asked, "Have you ever stolen anything from the warehouse?" His response is, "I'm the Operations Manager" as if that position would preclude the possibility of wrongdoing. He equates position and character. By virtue of his position, one should assume he is of good character.

Rationalization

Under this category of defense mechanisms I want to reiterate what I said previously; that people who commit wrongdoings will justify the act at the time it is committed or they will later seek to justify it to put themselves in a better light. Rationalization comes into play primarily after a person admits being involved in wrongdoing but gives a face-saving reason for the crime as opposed to telling the real motive.

In sex cases, they blame the victim. They make such statements as:

1. "She was looking for it. She wasn't forced."
2. "I know she's young but she was coming on to me."
3. "She was the first one to do anything."
4. "I was just trying to teach her."
5. "She's always flirting with her male playmates."
6. "She exposes herself."
7. "I was nice to her. I gave her presents and money."

In commercial thefts, the thief will find a real or imagined grievance to justify stealing from the employer. He will complain about being underpaid, working long hours or having an abusive boss. When I think about rationalization, I am reminded of the joke where a defendant accused of a stabbing claimed in court, "I was just standing on the corner peeling an apple when this guy backed into me sixteen times." In fraud cases, where a victim has been duped, the accused will frequently use the excuse that the victim was greedy.

In murder cases, you often hear the contention that "I never had any intention of killing her but then she threatened to get even with me. That made me angry. I didn't want her to be a witness against me." It's important to understand that the guilty have to go on living with themselves. In all human beings, there is a driving need for self-respect. No matter how heinous the crime, in time the perpetrator will find someway to project his guilt and rationalize the act.

Disassociation

From the interrogation of thousands of people, I am convinced that the brain has the ability to tranquilize itself. This explains the dispassionate demeanor displayed by people after they commit a crime. The mind tries to come to grips with the enormity of the act committed and appears to put the individual in an emotionally neutral state.

You see the same demeanor with those individuals who have experienced a particularly traumatic event.

The guilty disassociate from the act committed by a "thinking-away" process. They are able to compartmentalize their mind so as not to display an emotion that might reveal their guilt. They give the impression of being unconcerned. They are not able to suppress the memory of the act committed, but they make a strong effort to suppress any emotional counterpart. You see signs of this particular defense mechanism as they avoid describing feelings. They will tell a story in a matter-of-fact way. They avoid words that could trigger an emotion such as "kill," "steal," etc. When they tell a story, they lack a realistic display of emotion that should match their words.

I once tested a young lady who borrowed her boyfriend's vehicle to leave her school and go home for lunch. On her way home she went through a red light and killed two elderly people in another vehicle. She claimed to the police that her light was green. The accident scene analysis raised doubts as to her contention. She was brought to me to see if she was telling the truth. During the pre-test Interview, I became convinced that she was lying because she never displayed the emotion of anger toward the victims, that she would have if they had in fact gone through a red light and jeopardized her life. When I pointed this out to her after the test, she confessed that she had in fact gone through the red light. If she had been telling the truth all along, she should have said to me, "Those crazy people almost killed me."

Those who disassociate are much more comfortable discussing peripheral matters that have nothing to do with their actual guilt or innocence. They spend long periods of time talking about matters prior to or after the time of the crime. They go into great detail in areas where they are safe, but gloss over the crucial time period when the act was committed. They keep their story tight because by doing this there's less ground to defend. They don't want to give you anything to analyze.

I've tested a lot of traveling jewelry salesmen who claim they were robbed. Some of them attempt to defraud the insurance company with a false claim. It's interesting to note that the common denominator in those making a false claim is the tightness of their story. The story is generally, " I felt something like a gun at the back of my neck and then they grabbed my valise containing the jewelry."

The liar rarely gives any description as to the height, weight or age of the robber, nor does he give an opinion as to whether the robber was white, Black or Hispanic. He generally says, "It happened so fast I can't tell you what happened." Most importantly he never describes feelings, in comparison to the truthful claimant who generally states something like, "My God, I almost defecated in my pants. I thought he was going to kill me."

The most frustrating tactic an interrogator can encounter is a suspect who disassociates by using repeated assertion. No matter what evidence you use to confront him, he'll just keep saying, "I didn't do it." He will not discuss the case or give any story outlining his defense. He just keeps repeating. "I didn't do it." He subscribes to the philosophy that it's easier to believe a lie one has heard a hundred times than to believe the truth one is hearing for the first time. Those who disassociate use the testimony of others in an effort to confirm their innocence. For example, when asked a direct question, "Why do you think your daughter is saying you molested her?" he responds, "All of her friends say that she is a liar." The guilty actually emphasize the testimony of others over their own.

Closely akin is the tactic of lying by referral. An example of this would be when you say to the suspect, "I'd like to go over where you were yesterday at 3:00 p.m." and he replies, "Oh, do I have to go over that again, that's contained in the statement I gave yesterday." He might also refer you to another individual to get the answer. This is lying by referral. He prefers to rest on the lie previously told than to repeat it in your presence.

Guilty people using disassociation will even deliberately fail to remember things that are not threatening to them. This bolsters their contention that they don't recall specific things regarding the incident in question. They try to give the impression that they have a bad memory and are not lying. There are times when fear actually does affect memory. A suspect who is afraid his guilt will be revealed is so contaminated by fear that he can't think straight. Whether the suspect's memory is faulty by design or because of fear, the inability to recall even the most obvious things is generally a sign of deception. It should be noted that when first confronted, an innocent person may be unable to recall every specific detail. The difference is that the innocent suspect will eventually remember.

Those employing the defense mechanism of disassociation will sometimes reveal indirectly why they're not telling the truth. For example, you will hear such statements as, "If I'm convicted of the crime I'll lose my license to practice medicine." Or, "If I'm convicted of this it will kill my wife." An experienced interrogator, after hearing such statements recognizes a significant barrier to the suspect confessing.

Another sign of disassociation is a suspect who employs the tactic of whistling in the graveyard. The suspect will put on an air of nonchalance by whistling or humming. He tries to give the appearance of being unconcerned about the accusations against him. On occasion, a suspect will laugh or tell jokes as a release of tension. This is an obvious feigned lack of concern as it is inappropriate for the suspect to be in that kind of mood considering the circumstances.

Those employing the defense mechanism of disassociation are masters of exclusion. Test by questioning how far they will go to exclude themselves from any physical or mental connection to the crime. For example:

1. "Do you know who committed the act?"
2. "Do you suspect anyone?"
3. "Have you ever fantasized about committing a similar act?"
4. "Have you ever heard or read about a similar act?"

Guilty people will generally respond "no" to all of these questions and exclude themselves to the point of absurdity.

I once tested a construction worker who was accused of flashing his penis at a woman in a real estate office. His construction office was in the same shopping center. He contended that the accusation was absurd and that he had never at any time walked by the real estate office. I knew the shopping center and recalled that there was a restaurant at the corner. I asked the construction worker if in the three years that he had been in the shopping center he had ever gone to the restaurant. He became very subdued because he knew that to get to that restaurant he had to walk right past the real estate office. He knew then that he had overextended himself in declaring that he had never walked past the real estate office. Moments later he confessed. Watch for sweeping declarations of exclusion.

The suspect trying to disassociate and come to grips with what he has done may ask, "How could I have done it?" Sometimes this question is posed to put the interrogator on the defense and other times it's asked by someone seeking help to understand himself. If the interrogator shows insight and empathy and gives the suspect a logical answer to the question, he can induce a confession. This happened to me while testing a young man in Tucson, Arizona, concerning the death of two young girls and the disappearance of another. The suspect stated, "You keep saying that I did it. Tell me why." I replied, "If I tell you why you killed these three girls will you tell me that you did it?" He said, "Yes." I then went into a somewhat lengthy dissertation about his aberrant sexual needs. When I finished he said, "You're right. Call in the attorney and I'll tell you about it." The next day, adding to his promise, he called in the press and made a full disclosure recounting the murders and identifying the location of the missing body.

Disassociation is sometimes masochistic in nature. Even if the suspect would be better off telling the truth than lying, he continues to disassociate. I've seen this many times when I've offered a suspect a chance to be a witness rather than a defendant. They are so angry at themselves they will refuse a good deal giving the impression they're cutting off their nose to spite their face. Freud contended that there is a death wish in many human beings. I believe that, and have observed it over the years watching suspects as they continue to lie when telling the truth would be to their advantage.

Sometimes those employing the defense mechanism of disassociation will change their story when confronted with irrefutable evidence concerning one point in the story. The suspect will concede the point to appear objective and to avoid looking like a complete liar. There is a saying that when you "lie about the part, you lie about the whole." In my opinion, that saying only applies when the suspect lies about something that was not worth lying about. The innocent suspect will sometimes lie about a detail because it may be embarrassing to him. For example, a man may lie about his whereabouts because he was out with a woman other than his wife. However, as a rule, innocent people don't change their story because they know what actually happened.

Projection

Every tactic employed under the umbrella of the defense mechanism of projection is based on revenge. The guilty do not like being accused because it places them in a subservient position. To level the playing field and out of revenge, they project their guilt outwardly onto others or to society in general.

Aside from evasiveness, hostility is the second most evident demeanor manifested by guilty people. There's an old saying, "You hate what you fear." The guilty are angry that they're put in a position of having to defend themselves. Out of revenge, they put on a contrived show of being offended. They act as if they're being unjustly accused. They do this to invoke guilt feelings in the interrogator. It's a means of achieving dominance and putting the interrogator in a subservient position. The innocent suspect will sometimes also express anger at being accused, but the anger will dissipate as he recognizes the objectivity of the interrogator. The innocent suspect will then willingly move on to a discussion of the case facts whereas the guilty suspect will maintain the air of hostility throughout the interview.

Utilizing the defense mechanism of projection the guilty suspect takes a negative situation and attempts to turn it into a positive one by making himself a victim rather than a perpetrator. By doing this, the suspect attempts to gain sympathy and recognition as the victim of a miscarriage of justice. The tactic of the accused is to create an element of doubt to take away the assertiveness of the interrogator. If the interrogator shows that he doubts the validity of what the suspect is saying, the suspect infers that he lacks objectivity and does not possess the intellect to discern the truth. The guilty suspect employing the defense mechanism of projection will often attempt to put the interrogator down and create an acrimonious environment thus giving him an excuse to walk out of the interrogation.

A type of suspect who uses the defense mechanism of projection is one whom I call the *plausible story-maker*. This particular suspect doesn't believe that confession is good for the soul. He can't stand to be put down or to lose the debate. He believes that by admitting his wrongdoing he loses his manliness and can't stand the idea of appearing stupid for having committed the act in question. He decides that no matter how preposterous his fabricated story, he is better off being accused of lying than confessing and eliminating all doubt as to his guilt. His crafted story is a sadistic tool to fight back and frustrate his accusers. His made-up story may be an insult to the intelligence of the interrogator, but the accused convinces himself that the story is plausible. If he tells the story often enough, and keeps refining it, he gets to the point where he almost believes it himself. This helps him put on an act of simulated innocence.

The plausible story-maker capitalizes on other possible explanations for the existence of physical and circumstantial evidence and witness testimony against him. He comes up with some explanation for each. He often succeeds because there are many people who believe that a person is not guilty if he doesn't confess. As previously stated, human beings are very good at lying, but terrible at detecting lies. The plausible story-maker knows this. You can spot the contrived story because the suspect oversells it, and tries too hard to convince. The story sounds rehearsed. The suspect perceives no inconsistencies in his own story. The story is actually more convincing in his mind than in yours. The suspect gets subdued when he realizes that you're not buying his story. The plausible story-maker is generally an articulate individual who doesn't like losing a debate. He contrives a bogus story because he thinks that if he doesn't try to explain the incriminating evidence, his guilt will be obvious. Often, the plausible story-maker creates a story to satisfy loved ones to help them in their desire to believe he is innocent.

I frequently travel to various jails and prisons to test inmates who claim that they were wrongly accused or convicted. It is in this environment that I see the most dramatic use of the defense mechanism of projection. Many of these individuals will argue a "legal innocence" vs. an absolute innocence. They believe that if their rights were violated in any way, either by the police or by the prosecutor, that automatically makes them legally innocent. They will find any excuse to project their guilt on either the police or the prosecutor. They prefer to argue about the conduct of the police or prosecutor rather than discussing the case facts. On the other hand, the innocents do not project guilt, and are willing to discuss the case facts. If it's a question of validity of the identification, I will often ask the inmate, "Do you think the witness lied about you?" The guilty are quick to project their guilt and respond, "Yes, I do." In contrast, the innocent will generally respond, "No, I think they really believe it was me. They're just mistaken."

There is a Latin phrase, *argumentum hominem*, which means discredit the man and you discredit his testimony. Some suspects do this to direct suspicion away from themselves. They will use overkill to undermine the credibility of a witness, or to direct suspicion toward another person. If they know something negative about a witness or other possible suspect, even though it has no bearing, they will capitalize on what they know to undermine the credibility of the witness, and direct more suspicion toward another suspect.

With projection, the liar will sometimes employ the well-known Red Herring Technique. He will attempt to force you to debate an aspect of the case that has nothing to do with his actual guilt or innocence. An engineer was suspected of a hit-and-run accident that resulted in the death of a woman who was crossing Flagler Street half a block from my office. The police got a lead, and picked up the engineer, who denied being involved, but there was suspicious damage to his Volkswagen. He was brought to my office for a polygraph test. The police told the engineer they had witness testimony that his vehicle was traveling at least 80 miles per hour at the time of the accident. The engineer's whole defense, before and after the polygraph test, was the fact that his vehicle was not capable of going 80 miles per hour because of an operational problem. After a while, I got tired of arguing about how fast his Volkswagen could travel, and in exasperation I said, "I don't really give a damn how fast your Volkswagen can go, and maybe you're right, but you were the driver of the vehicle who killed the woman." Happy that at last he won one point, he replied, "Yes, I was."

When you do a lot of work for family court, and particularly in child custody cases, you find out that those who lie out of revenge are much more convincing than those who lie out of fear. Both spouses tell convincing stories, although they are diametrically opposed, one has to be lying. Discerning which one is lying is not easily accomplished. The one who is lying justifies the lie based on a real or imagined grievance, and his hatred is so intense that it supersedes his fear of detection.

I once read that group protection is considered, by some, to be a greater virtue than lying to a person in a position of authority is a vice. I have, on numerous occasions, been up against that type of thinking. Some minority group members will project their guilt toward the interrogator because he is not a member of their group. They think stonewalling is a noble endeavor. In the chapter "Accusatory Interrogation," I will discuss how to counteract this view.

The defense mechanism of projection is seen particularly in cases involving interrogations concerning confrontations which have led to mayhem. The person lying does so out of hatred. He would rather suffer the consequences of his act, than admit the truth and give his adversary a victory. People who have committed inside thefts, often use the defense mechanism of projection. They project their guilt by opening up the crime to the world. The suspect may say, "The safe door was left ajar, and the manager's office was left unattended. Several people went into the office to use the phone or pick up supplies." None of this actually happened, but the person who stole the money uses these statements to divert suspicion from himself.

Some suspects utilize the defense mechanism of projection to put the interrogator on the defensive, and preempt the interrogation by claiming they were subjected to third degree tactics by previous interrogators. This is done to undermine the assertiveness of the interrogator.

THE NEUROTIC LIAR AND THE PSYCHOPATH

The Neurotic Liar

I'm not sure about the label for this type of liar, but I've always said, "Give me a person who lies to me and I have a chance of getting a confession. But give me a person who lies to himself and I have no chance." With the neurotic liar you get the impression that they are saying to themselves, "I can't be guilty of this act." This is different from saying to oneself, "I did it and I'm going to lie about it."

To the neurotic liar, the truth is too threatening to their psyche. By lying to themselves, they maintain a semblance of mental balance, which makes life halfway tolerable. Generally speaking, their personality structure is too weak to accept the fact that they committed any wrongdoing. Any admission of wrongdoing may lead to suicide or psychosis. There is a consensus of opinion that neurotic behavior is based on self-deception. The experienced interrogator can spot the neurotic by his somewhat bewildered and frenzied demeanor. Oddly enough, despite their instability they can plug illogical loopholes in their story with plausible explanations. To protect their psyche they are well-practiced in this ability.

I once tested a female shoplifter who, according to her psychologist, suffered from a "free-floating anxiety." Unable to understand her constant anxiety, she committed the act of shoplifting to give her something tangible to feel guilty about. I had a difficult time getting her to tell the truth. Finally, I gave up and told her to leave. She looked at me and said, "I think you should talk to me some more." I realized then that the interrogation was therapeutic and was abating her guilt feelings. She finally told the truth but only after a lot of handholding.

When fantasy becomes the substitute for reality, the neurotic liar may not manifest signs of lying because he believes what he says. It's interesting to note that the neurotic liar tells a fantasy story which often includes so many details that the interrogator may make the mistake of thinking that no one could have possibly made up that much.

The Psychopath/Sociopath

The suspect who fascinates me the most is the psychopath. Twenty percent of prisoners are classified as psychopaths. Some academics call them sociopaths. Those who believe in the influence of heredity call them psychopaths. Those who believe that nurture has the strongest influence call them sociopaths. Personally, I believe there is a genetic basis to this type of personality. As a school administrator, my daughter has told me that she has seen a cluster of these traits in children as young as five and that the profile is full-blown by fourth grade. I've spent a considerable amount of time studying the works of Dr. David Lykken, Dr. Robert Hare, Dr. Wiley (from England), and more recently, Dr. J. Ogloff and Dr. S. Wong concerning psychopaths. They all attribute almost the same characteristics to the psychopath.

Not all psychopaths are in prison. Many function in society and never go to prison. Obviously, the following characteristics are found in the general population. The psychopath is distinguishable in that he represents the extreme embodiment of these characteristics:

1. No conscience. No guilt feelings.
2. Lacks empathy.
3. Has no feelings for others.
4. Impulsive, lives for the present.
5. Glib and articulate.
6. Great social skills.
7. Control and/or power freaks.
8. Obsessed with recognition.
9. Prolific liar.
10. Egocentric, has grandiose ideas about himself.
11. Excitement junkies.
12. Narcissistic.
13. Inflated view of self-worth.
14. Braggart.
15. Arrogant.

16. Opinionated.
17. Domineering.
18. No sense of embarrassment when caught lying.
19. Proud of his ability to lie.
20. Manipulative.
21. Hates criticism.
22. Does not have a normal range of emotions. Hair-trigger temper.
23. Higher rate of recidivism than other criminals.

Early Signs of Psychopathy in Children

1. Persistent lying.
2. Stealing.
3. Fire-setting.
4. Truancy.
5. Persistent class disruption.
6. Substance abuse.
7. Cruelty to animals.
8. Vandalism.
9. Bullying/manipulation.
10. Running away.

I don't disagree with any of these characteristics as listed by the doctors. I have tested hundreds of psychopaths and would like to add my observations to what has already been said.

This type of personality always moves forward during the interview invading your life space. When they enter my office, they practically jump in my secretary's lap. They are quick to overpower with a firm handshake and supercilious smile. When they sit down they invariably pick up their chair and move it closer to you. They lean into you when they're talking. In a show of intimacy they will pick up something like a pen from your desk and tap it there as they make their point. They do this as if to say, "See, I'm not scared of you. If I was, I wouldn't get this close."

No one stares like a psychopath. They maintain intense eye contact in an effort to dominate. They try to control the conversation by talking quickly making it difficult to ask questions. They are masters of interpersonal relations because good liars are good at sizing-up people. A psychopath will tell such a mind-boggling story that you can't believe it could be made up. There is one flaw in their storytelling that can save an interrogator from being fooled. They fail to document their stories with real people, full names, or full and correct addresses. They never provide any type of documentation to verify their stories. When you press them for verification, you get the sensation that you are struggling with a slippery snake. When you catch them in a lie, they show no embarrassment. They just keep talking as if nothing happened.

One of the best indicators that you have a psychopath is that they must dominate and can't take no for an answer. After the polygraph test, if you tell them they're lying, you have to practically throw them out of the office to get rid of them. They will keep on talking to you to get you to change your mind.

MISCELLANEOUS TACTICS OF THE LIAR

Some tactics used by liars are not categorized within a specific defense mechanism but are used in conjunction with one. One of the most obvious tactics of the liar is his use of "statements to convince."

Statements to Convince

Statements to convince are used to reduce a person's defense down to a single utterance which in the suspect's mind cannot be refuted. This type of liar lacks the creativity to craft a plausible story. These sound like:

1. "I don't need to steal. I get all the money I need from my grandmother."
2. "There was no reason for me to burn my business down. I was making money."
3. "Why would I rape some woman? I get all the sex I want at home."

When a person makes a statement to convince, he assumes that you will accept his contention as a matter of fact. The suspect has analyzed his situation and he believes that the statement to convince is the best thing he can say to defend himself. He will continue to repeat that particular assertion until it is refuted by the interrogator. It is imperative that the interrogator knock out the statement to convince or the suspect will continue to ride that horse.

Statements to convince come out of left field and are not made in response to an interrogator's question. You get the impression that the suspect couldn't wait to make the statement to test the interrogator's reaction. The litmus test to determine if it is a statement to convince or just a remark made by an innocent person is to see how far the suspect will go to defend the validity of the contention. For example, if the suspect does not concede that his grandmother would draw the line at some request for money, then that is a good indication that the statement was a lie. The best way to handle statements to convince is to point out the absurdity of the contention.

"It's Impossible. . . ." In commercial cases, the person responsible for the theft will use the tactic that it is impossible to steal from the place where he works. To mislead the interrogator he will even describe the company's security measures. By claiming that nobody could steal from the company, he is attempting to automatically exclude himself from suspicion.

"You Don't Understand. . . ." When you try to make the suspect be more explicit and the suspect doesn't want to go into detail, it is because the details will reveal his guilt. He will summarily dismiss the interrogator by saying that, "If I explained it you wouldn't understand it anyway." This statement is generally made by people who are part of a subculture that has its own created language. Watch for this tactic in cases of computer fraud, fraudulent sophisticated business activities, within the drug culture, or in cults.

The Lazy Liar

A lie generally follows the path of least resistance. Often the liar is too lazy to be creative. He will tell a story using the same names, colors and particulars. By doing this, he has less to remember. Too many different descriptions might trip him up in the retelling of his story.

The Narrow Denial

Liars deny things specifically. Innocent people deny things inclusively. I learned this testing a porter who was accused of killing his boss's wife. She was found dead after being raped and strangled in the storage area of her store. The homicide investigators and I assumed that the ligature used in the strangulation was a piece of mattress ticking found near her neck. After several hours of interrogation, I decided to take a rest and let the homicide investigators take over the interrogation. As I watched from the observation room, I heard the suspect say several times, "I didn't kill any woman with a piece of cloth." It suddenly dawned on me that he wasn't denying the crime, he was denying the implement of the crime. I went back into the interrogation room and asked the homicide investigators to leave. I looked at the suspect and said, "All of this time you've been right and we've been wrong. You didn't use the cloth. What *did* you use?" He looked at me calmly and stated, "I used an electrical cord and put it in a box." I learned from that case that if you have the case facts wrong that justifies a suspect's denial and he's not going to give you the satisfaction of hearing him confess until you get them right.

In commercial cases, the accused will deny stealing a specific amount of money. The innocent on the other hand, will state, "I didn't steal $158 or any other amount of money from the register." Be leery of suspects who do not deny things inclusively. A person responsible for a series of acts will sometimes admit one but not the others. His motive is to minimize his guilt and not look too bad. He will say, "I've admitted one, if I did the others why wouldn't I admit them?" That sounds convincing but many times, it is a spurious argument. I once tested a young man who had committed eight murders from California to Florida. It took me two days to get him to admit to all eight murders. When I asked him why he didn't admit all eight at one time he said, "I didn't want to be tried in all those different places." Sometimes the motive for not admitting additional acts is inexplicable but it still has to be ferreted out by the interrogator.

The Smart Liar

The smart liar admits everything that you can prove and nothing that you can't prove. He does this so you can't accuse him of being a liar. The smart liar will also make minor admissions to appear truthful. For example, he will state, "I didn't steal a thousand dollars but I once took fifty dollars." This tactic is employed to give the impression that the suspect has credibility by making an admission even if it's minor. In fact, it is done to mislead the interrogator and just give him a piece of the cake.

The Icing on the Cake

In a last ditch effort to convince the interrogator, many liars will mention significant facts at the end of the interrogation or as they walk out the door. It's an obvious lie to support their position because anything significant should have been mentioned up front or early in the interview. An innocent person would never leave out a detail if it were true and important.

Let Me Correct That

Liars who tell a crafted story will often make corrections to give the impression that they want to be exact and therefore must be telling the truth. They will make statements like, "Oh, I'm sorry. It wasn't Tuesday, it was Wednesday" and "I'm sorry. I'm wrong in that. It was around 2:30 rather than 4:30." The liar will also add incidental details or individuals to lend credibility to his story, but when you try to pin him down, what was added can't be confirmed. You never get a full name or a complete address.

BODY LANGUAGE

When I first became a polygraph examiner, the first thing I noticed, from a subjective standpoint, was the remarkable similarity in how people lied. Most notable, were the similar remarks they made, the essence of their stories and the defense mechanisms they employed. What the suspects had to say and how they said it, occupied all of my attention. By choice, my subjective analysis zeroed in on the spoken word, and not body language. In interpreting body language, I've had difficulty in distinguishing the difference between a nervous guilty and a nervous innocent. When I get around to accusing a suspect of lying, I'm more comfortable basing that opinion on the polygraph test results and the inconsistencies in the suspect's story as opposed to the fact that the suspect was tapping his fingers throughout the interrogation session. When a suspect says to me, "Mr. Holmes, I didn't steal the money, but I feel morally obligated to pay it back," I'm more apt to believe that that particular suspect is lying based on that remark, than the fact that he may have been tapping his fingers during the interview.

There have been some excellent books and articles written about body language. They have, in my opinion, one thing in common; the conclusion that all body language reflects an emotion, and by interpreting the body language, one can tell which emotion is being reflected. The interrogator has to deal primarily with two emotions, fear and anger. Both of these emotions are generally discernible in the body language of a suspect. There is, however, no absolute correlation between body language and lying. The absence of an absolute correlation does not negate the fact that the interpretation of body language can be a valuable adjunct in determining deception.

Although I have placed more emphasis on the spoken word than body language, I have noted a sufficient correlation between body language indicators and those who later confessed. This indicator was the fear I saw in the suspect's eyes revealed by the dilation in the pupils of the suspect's eyes. One gets the impression that the intensity of the suspect's fear seems centered in his eyes.

Innocent people generally sound and look like they are telling the truth. I think part of that innocent appearance is based on the fact that they don't break eye contact. Many students of body language believe that breaking eye contact is a typical behavior of liars. It's been my experience that many shy people do the same thing. Sociopaths are clever enough not to reveal themselves by breaking eye contact. In fact, in their effort to simulate innocence, they try to stare a hole in the interrogator. Their use of a penetrating stare is an effort to achieve dominance in the interrogation session.

It is my opinion that for the purpose of detecting deception, any body movement based on the big muscles of the body is more significant than those movements controlled by the small muscles. General noticed tension is evident by finger movement, foot tapping, etc. These movements are controlled by the small muscles, and you see these movements present in both the nervous guilty and nervous innocent. By comparison, if the liar is caught off guard by a decisive question such as, "Did you steal the $1,000?" or "Did you shoot Harry Brown?" the big muscles come into play. Frequently, you will see the liar swing one leg over the other, or shift his entire body weight in his chair.

Observing body language, case analysis, plus the interpretation of a suspect's story and remarks is an eclectic approach to lie detection. Anything that can lead to a definitive conclusion as to guilt or innocence has value. If the interrogator doesn't have confidence in the suspect's guilt, the suspect senses that element of doubt, and that will increase the suspect's resolve to resist.

Chapter V

WHY PEOPLE DON'T CONFESS
AND WHY THEY DO

Before you begin your specific interrogations, you should have some general knowledge as to why people don't confess and why they do. From the general background information and the biographical data of the suspect you're going to interrogate, you should have some insight as to why the particular suspect may not confess and why he might. In fact, it's a good idea to write down a game plan. You should list the specific roadblocks to be countered and you should also list the mitigating factors that might prompt the suspect to confess. You just can't go into an interrogation room assuming you can wing it. If you are ill prepared, you might negate the opportunity to get a confession that could have been obtained with preparation.

The reasons why people don't confess fall under two main categories: practical and psychological. The practical reasons for not confessing are:

1. Fear of going to jail.
2. Fear of being killed or suffering bodily harm from a co-defendant.
3. Fear of losing one's job/business or pension.
4. Fear of losing one's professional license (medical, legal, etc).
5. Fear of losing one's life-style.
6. Reluctance to involve a loved one (brother, spouse, etc).
7. Fear of embarrassing family members.
8. Reluctance to give up the fruits of the crime.
9. Fear of opening up the door to the investigation of other crimes they have committed.

10. Suspect has been told by a lawyer not to confess.
11. Reluctance to involve co-defendants (playing the martyr by protecting someone else).
12. Suspect is convinced there is insufficient evidence to get a conviction.

The psychological reasons for not confessing are:

1. Bad interrogation environment; too many people around.
2. Suspect does not trust the interrogator.
3. Suspect doesn't want to experience the shame of being guilty.
4. Suspect feels he will lose his manliness by confessing because confessing will put him in a subservient position to the interrogator.
5. Suspect does not want to give up his weapon of revenge, which is to create doubt as to his guilt; and gets a sadistic delight by not confessing.
6. The case is his claim to fame and he enjoys the celebrity status that could be diminished by an admission of guilt.
7. Suspect's overriding ego negates his acceptance of guilt, it is too humiliating to confess, and he doesn't want to destroy his self-image by admitting guilt.
8. Suspect has been a prolific liar all his life, and doesn't tell the truth about anything. He constantly lies to increase his self-worth, thus a confession would undermine his whole existence. He hates all forms of authority–parents, school, church, police. Therefore, to confess would be tantamount to surrender.
9. Interrogator has the case facts wrong, suspect will not confess until he gets them right.
10. Suspect is masochistic in nature, wants to "cut off his nose to spite his face" even if a confession would be to his advantage.
11. Suspect is enjoying the role as victim of an alleged injustice as the "falsely accused" rather than the perpetrator.
12. Suspect doesn't want to give his adversary a victory by confessing (business partner, rival, wife, etc).
13. Compensatory mechanism for low IQ; suspect is trying to hide his ignorance and by lying becomes the smartest one in the room because he knows the truth and the interrogator doesn't.
14. Suspect cannot remember the precise details of the crime because of the influence of drugs or alcohol and starts to think that maybe he didn't commit the crime.

15. Suspect is embarrassed by the crime because he possesses an expertise that should exclude him from such minimal acts (safe cracker picked up for shoplifting).
16. Suspect committed a benevolent act during the crime that, in his mind, negates his guilt.

Why People Do Confess

There are both practical and psychological reasons why people do confess. The practical reasons are:

1. The resignation factor: The suspect realizes there is too much evidence against him.
2. The self-interest principle: To get a lesser penalty/better deal, become a witness rather than a perpetrator.

The psychological reasons are:

1. Institutionalized to prison life, not fearful of going to prison, happier inside than out.
2. Torture–More confessions are obtained worldwide by torture than by any other means. The U.S. and a few other nations are the only ones that demand reasonable methods of inquiry.
3. Psychological duress–Long periods of interrogation will wear down a suspect's resistance to a point where he eventually confesses to get the interrogator off his back.
4. Revenge–Confesses to embarrass a loved-one (father, wife, etc).
5. Vicarious thrill–Desires to relive the crime to enjoy the same sensual feelings experienced at the time of the crime; telling another person or the interrogator heightens the reliving of the sensual experience.
6. Masochism–Confesses to insure punishment.
7. Restoration factor–The confession is an effort to regain personal and public respect and acceptance; the subject tells himself, "Why be a liar on top of what I've already done." Subject is looking to be recognized as a good person who simply made a mistake.
8. Succumbs to the entreaties of his family.
9. The act is so bizarre that he is hoping someone else will give him insight as to why he did it.
10. The influence of religious teachings.

11. The pain of conscience–Some technicians of the law believe that the only valid confession is one given voluntarily because of the pain of conscience. This concept assumes that guilt feelings are so intolerable that they can provoke the average person to confess for alleviation. If this concept is true, why do we have 6,000 unsolved murders in this country each year? Why aren't these murderers knocking down the doors of the police stations to confess? It is my opinion that most people can live with guilt abated by various defense mechanisms. Guilt is a private thing. What people cannot live with is shame, based on public exposure.

It has been my experience that people confess out of the self-interest principle rather than being goaded into it by a stricken conscience. Frankly, I don't believe anybody really knows what conscience is. I've read all kinds of theories from Freud's super-ego to the belief by some psychologists that conscience is developed by a conditioning process which inculcates mores. I've included the concept of conscience in this list of reasons why people confess because I can't disprove it.

12. The Interrogator–Many years ago, I worked on a case where a porter murdered the female manager of a Western Union Office in Palm Beach, Florida. She caught him stealing money from an open safe and he picked up a stick near the safe and bludgeoned her to death. The Palm Beach authorities told me that they only had one witness who saw the porter leave the office at the time of the murder. They said that they absolutely had to have a confession in order to convict.

After the polygraph examination, the suspect confessed to me that he killed the woman. I watched him die in the electric chair. On the way home the sheriff said to me, "If you hadn't gotten that confession we wouldn't have seen what we saw today." That experience, more than any other, brought to my mind the powerful influence of the Interrogator and persuasive arguments in obtaining confessions. No other factor besides irrefutable evidence has more of a bearing in obtaining a confession than the Interrogator.

I read once that if the German people had read Hitler's speeches instead of hearing him deliver them in person that they would never have followed him into war. Speech is more emotive than the printed word. It can stir the emotions like music, art or poetry. It's difficult to understand why we are so susceptible to speech. You have to ask yourself how a man like Hitler came to power primarily based on his speaking ability. How does a cult leader convince hundreds of followers to commit mass suicide? Why do we fall under the spell of a salesperson? Why does a person confess to an act of murder because of the words an interrogator strings together? I don't know the answers to all of these questions but naturally I have given considerable thought to this phenomenon as it pertains to interrogation.

Boiling it all down I think the answer lies in the subject's need for recognition. In my opinion, people are recognition junkies. From the time they come out of the womb humans have an insatiable appetite for attention and recognition. An interrogation session is probably the most unique interpersonal relationship that can take place between two human beings. Out of diverse interests, an intimacy is created, symbiotic in nature. The interrogator wants the confession and the subject wants understanding. The attention the subject gets is intoxicating to him.

When I was on the Miami Police Department jailers would frequently call to tell me that a suspect wanted to talk to me again. The jailer would add, "He said he would make it worth your while." I didn't understand why after several hours of interrogation the suspect would want to see me again. After this happened several times, it became obvious that the suspect was feeding on the attention he was getting, and the interrogation session was satisfying his need for recognition. Many murder suspects will confess to reward the Interrogator for his patience, attention and understanding. It is difficult to conceive that a person would confess because of some psychological need in spite of the potential consequences of confessing, but that is exactly what happens. There are few times in a suspect's life where he gets such intense attention from another human being as in an interrogation session. It is mesmerizing to the suspect. Many suspects love the audience. As an interrogator, it pays to be a good listener. Some suspects confess just to prolong the attention of the interrogator.

Overall Guidelines for Interrogational Arguments

The practical and psychological reasons for not confessing and confessing suggest certain overall guidelines for interrogational arguments or themes.

1. Any argument you create must not insult the intelligence of the suspect. The argument should appeal to the suspect's common sense. It should offer a realistic solution to his problem. If the argument is obvious malarkey, the suspect will lose respect for the interrogator. Suspects do not confess to people they don't respect.
2. Every created argument has to have a truthful basis.
3. The argument should show insight. The interrogator should give the impression that he understands the suspect's problem and what he fears. Showing insight is one of the better methods for the interrogator to ingratiate himself with the suspect.
4. Arguments must not be demeaning to the ego of the suspect. If you make "an animal" out of the suspect, he's not going to give you the satisfaction of hearing him confess. You have to leave him with some dignity because he has to go on living with himself.
5. The arguments should address and counter roadblocks to confession specific to the person being interrogated.
6. The arguments should capitalize on any mitigating factors likely to induce the suspect to confess.

In the following pages, I will discuss specific crimes and suggested interrogational approaches.

Chapter VI

THE TRANSITION FROM NONACCUSATORY INTERROGATION TO ACCUSATORY INTERROGATION

The transition from nonaccusatory interrogation to accusatory interrogation is simple for a polygraph examiner. All he has to do is to lay out the polygraph charts and then tell the suspect that they show he is not telling the truth. The polygraph examiner then states that he kept an open mind until he saw the test results. The examiner points out that the test results corroborate the validity of the evidence and the witness testimony against the suspect. He then launches immediately into accusatory interrogation.

Without polygraph test results, the interrogator is in a much more difficult position as he makes the transition from nonaccusatory to accusatory interrogation. There is however, a way of doing this if the interrogator is convinced that the suspect is lying based on his story or the answers to the interrogator's questions. It should be pointed out that if there is an element of doubt as to the suspect's guilt the interrogator has to make the transition in a manner that will leave him with a bail-out position. The interrogator has to avoid the embarrassment of accusing an innocent person of lying. To avoid alienating an innocent person while making the transition I suggest the following spiel.

Interrogator: "Ok, I've listened to your story and your answers to my questions and frankly I'm disturbed by some things. So, I want to talk to you on a hypothetical basis. I'm not positively assuming anything. But, let's just assume and again, I'm only talking hypothetically, that, as always you have been trying to steer your course in life, but lately things have changed beyond your control. Every time you get your head above water, someone pushes you under. You feel like everything you do is an exercise in futility. Perhaps you've gotten to a point where you don't care anymore. Under normal conditions you would never consider the act you are accused of, but in this 'I don't give a damn state of mind,' you might do something you wouldn't ordinarily do."

After completing these initial remarks, the interrogator should look for "buying signals" emanating from the suspect indicating that the suspect is weighing what the interrogator said. The first "buying signal" is that the suspect is listening intently to what the interrogator is saying; that he is obviously considering what has been said. Other "buying signals" are: the nodding of the head in assent, a slumping in posture, a more grim expression on the suspect's face, and primarily with females, a welling-up of tears in the eyes.

If the interrogator sees these signs, he should become more assertive in his approach. "Frankly, everything I know about you tells me that under sufficient stress you would in fact commit the act you are accused of." If the interrogator gets no response to that statement, he should move more strongly into accusatory interrogation. "I'm trying to be objective, but everything I know tells me that you did in fact commit this crime." If the suspect does not refute that statement strongly, the interrogator should then point out all of the reasons why he thinks the suspect is lying. Follow this with specific arguments or themes to persuade the suspect to confess.

If during the transition the suspect is vociferous in his denial and the interrogator gets the impression that the suspect is "looking good" and perhaps is innocent, the interrogator may then have to use the fall-back position. For example, "Listen, I told you before I started talking I wasn't assuming anything and that I was going to talk to you on a hypothetical basis. I can't cut open your head to see the truth. I have to consider all of the possibilities. If you were in my position in view of the circumstances, you would have doubts too."

That statement generally satisfies the wrongly accused. Ironically, you do not really see strong signs of innocence until you accuse a person of committing the crime. By comparison, the guilty do not become insulted when accused because they do not have their heart in defending their position.

THE CONFESSION FORMULA

In the early 1980s, I was reviewing some videotapes of interrogations I had conducted on various criminal suspects. I noticed something that I was doing out of habit that led me to my formulation of the confession formula. I saw that as, I presented what I thought were pretty good arguments as to why the suspect should tell the truth, I wasn't having much success. I noted however, that when I would suddenly get up from my chair, stand over the suspect and become sterner in demeanor, they would confess. It became obvious to me that they confessed because I became more assertive.

Suspects live in hope that they can lie to the interrogator successfully. They sometimes think the interrogator is bluffing and that he doesn't know the truth. They hope that the interrogator is going to lose patience and quit. They say to themselves, "If I can just outlast this guy I'll be all right."

The interrogator's change in body position, and his "I'm not going to take no for an answer" demeanor is usually psychologically devastating to the suspect. The suspect's little game of seeing how far he can go before he tells the truth is thwarted by the interrogator's increased assertiveness.

It became obvious to me that despite the interrogator's use of the evidence and persuasive arguments, in most instances this was not sufficient to induce a confession. What was needed was a more assertive declaration of guilt. Any presentation of arguments or themes done in an apologetic manner or tongue-in-check just would not do the job.

The increase in assertiveness works because the suspect doesn't want to alienate the interrogator or insult his intelligence. The interrogator's measured increase in assertiveness gets the job done without inducing false confessions. There is a basic difference between assertiveness and duress, which is prolonged in nature. Knowing these factors led me to the *confession formula*.

Leverage Plus the Force of the Assertion of Guilt Equals Confession

Leverage in any interrogation session is the weight and the amount of evidence you have to confront the suspect. There is a direct correlation between the weight and the amount of evidence you have and your chance of getting a confession. Irrefutable evidence is the ultimate leverage in any interrogation session.

The secret to successful interrogation is encompassed in the second part of the formula, the force of the assertion of guilt. The interrogator should continually increase the force of the assertion of guilt. He should do this with three levels of confrontation. First, confront the suspect with the evidence against him. Second, confront the suspect with powerful persuasive arguments. Third, dramatically raise the force of the assertion by changing body position and demeanor.

At the third level of confrontation it has to be obvious to the suspect that there is no longer a question of his innocence or guilt but of whether or not he has the fortitude to tell the truth. There is no doubt in my mind that most confessions come at the third level of confrontation.

There is a misconception in our society which is reinforced by some television shows, that all you have to do is confront the suspect, and he won't be able to wait to confess. When I left the Miami Police Department, I started to do a lot of polygraph testing for defense attorneys. I initially assumed that since the suspects knew the tests were confidential that it would be easy to get confessions. I soon found out differently. Eighty-five percent or more of clients lie to their own attorneys. Those who commit a wrongdoing are so ego-protective, that no matter who questions them they don't tell the truth. I also found out that people with no criminal background are just as tough to interrogate as those with felony records. There is a reason for this. With criminals, shame is not always a major factor. For the average person with no criminal record the fear of shame is a major roadblock. The second roadblock is their fear that a confession would end "life as they know it." Criminals on the other hand, don't have that much to lose.

THE THREE MAJOR TYPES OF INTERROGATIONAL ARGUMENTS

It has always been my opinion that all interrogational arguments fall into three major categories:

1. General Arguments–used for any type of crime.
2. Specific Arguments–used for a particular type of crime.
3. Situational Arguments–used because of a particular suspect's personality or the unique features of the crime; may be utilized only once in your career.

What follows are samples of each of the three types of interrogational arguments I have used to solve actual cases.

A General Argument

Now I want you to listen to me. The legal system in this country is based as much on psychology as it is on law. When you walk into the courtroom, you will face a judge who puts his pants on the same way you do. If you insult the intelligence of the judge or the jury, you may get more time for lying than for what you actually did. If you're smart you know that if you can't save all of your ass you should try to save at least half of it. Even a professional hood knows when to throw in the towel. I suggest to you that you don't want to 'rub the fur the wrong way.' The whole legal system is predicated on the basis that if you throw yourself on the mercy of the court you will invariably get a lesser penalty. Most judges believe that the first step in rehabilitation is for the person to acknowledge his guilt and show contrition, which simply means appearing sorry for what you did. You have the right to a trial but a trial means that you place yourself in an adversarial position with the state. It also means that you are a poor candidate for rehabilitation. Right now, you're thinking emotionally rather than rationally. It doesn't make any difference to me what you do because I get paid whether you confess or not. You also have to consider that what you think now may not be the way you think about this whole situation two years from now. I don't think you're going to be able to lie around the evidence presented against you in court. I think you should make the practical decision that what you did was bad enough, why be a liar on top of that? You know I'm right, don't you?

A Specific Argument for Incest Cases

Let me tell you something that you don't understand. Your daughter's accusation against you is bad enough but what you are doing right now by denying the act is even worse. The mind of a child your daughter's age is like a piece of silly-putty. It can be shaped in any direction. Right now, she needs fortification and assurance that she did the right thing in telling her mother what you did. When a child is telling the truth and the adults are saying that she's lying she can get to the point where she doubts her own mind. She could easily splinter off from reality and in that sense, you could have done irreparable harm to her by tearing her thought processes asunder. As men, we can't understand what these experiences mean to women or little girls. They can get over the uncomfortable feelings about the physical act, but what does the long-term emotional damage is the sense of betrayal and the loss of the ability to trust. It can keep a woman from being able to go on and have a happy marriage or be a good parent.

I do not think your daughter hates you, but even at her age she knows what you were doing was wrong. She probably feels guilty about taking part in what happened but her greatest fear right now is of losing your love and approval. If you make her out to be a liar, you risk incurring her hatred for the rest of your life. I don't think you meant to harm her in these ways. She needs you to tell her that she did the right thing. You have the alternative of suffering the momentary embarrassment of relating to me what you did or carrying the weight of this guilt for the rest of your life for creating an unstable personality in your child. You can rectify a bad situation for both of you by telling the truth and start rebuilding your relationship with your child. I think you have to muster up the fortitude to tell the truth and bring stability to your daughter's life. Now she is telling the truth, isn't she?

A Situational Argument

As you know I've been hired by the newspaper to test you and the former Chief of Police to determine which of you suppressed the report containing derogatory information regarding the Commonwealth Attorney. You claim that you gave the report to the Chief and he denies that fact. I'm convinced both in talking to you and testing you that you suppressed the report and never gave it to the Chief as you contend. By denying that act, you're making a bad situation worse. You're making it appear that you got paid money to suppress the report. That impression is damaging to you as a police captain but it also besmirches you family's good reputation in this community. I don't think you were paid to suppress the report, but that you suppressed the report to ingratiate yourself with the Commonwealth Attorney. You knew the Chief was going to retire and a recommendation from the Commonwealth Attorney would put you in a position to be appointed Chief. I'm going to flat out tell the newspaper people that I think you're lying and I don't think, since they paid for me to come all the way from Miami, that they're going to ignore what I have to say. I don't think you can afford to leave the inference hanging in the air that you took a buck to suppress that report. If you want to stop all of this lying and tell me the truth I'll bet my golf clubs you can pass another test on whether or not you took money. Now, you did suppress the report, didn't you?"

The captain replied yes and was retested solely on the issue to determine if he took money to suppress the report. It was my opinion that he told the truth in his denial of accepting any money for suppressing the report. In the pages that follow, I will discuss different crimes and suggest interrogational arguments best suited for each type.

Chapter VII

SEX CRIMES

A GENERAL THEORY FOR SEX CRIMES

A large portion of my career as a polygraph examiner involved testing people suspected of sex crimes. Over a period of time, it became apparent to me, that two factors in the sex drive were primarily responsible for sex crimes. Aggressiveness and the need for recognition satisfied by control of the victim. Aggression plays a vital role in the evolutionary process. It is the fuel that propels the evolutionary process. It is axiomatic that the propagation of the human species is dependent on heterosexual relations. To ensure the preservation of any species, there has to be a propelling force in males to ensure copulation and in my opinion, that force is aggression. In human and animal life, various degrees of aggression are an integral part of the sex act. Stoic males would lead to the demise of a species. Aggression therefore, as it pertains to sex, has social utility. The problem arises when aggression and its counterpart, sadism, becomes disproportionate to the simple biological and psychological need for orgasm. To the sexual offender, placing the penis in the vagina without intimidation is not what they enjoy. To the sexual offender, satisfying his sexual drive by socially acceptable means leaves his aberrant desires unfulfilled. To the sexual offender, the act has to mirror the excitement of his bizarre thought process.

In this chapter I use the term "sex offender" to differentiate from other criminals who commit such acts as burglary, armed robbery, etc. The truth is, most criminals, regardless of the method of operation, are sexual offenders. The criminal is the ultimate male chauvinist. Most of them have a disdain for women. I can assure you that if the aver-

64

age burglar or armed robber has the opportunity to commit rape, he will do it. The nature of their aggression is not different than the one possessed by the serial rapist. Most criminals possess a sadistic nature, wherein subjugating the victim is necessary to enhance the excitement of the sexual act.

I don't think that any human being is totally free of some degree of aggression, since we all are a byproduct of thousands of years of evolution. Natural selection is the outgrowth of aggression. In this respect, aggression has social utility in that it is the fuel for the evolutionary process, but aggression is also the bane of our existence, being that it is the underlying cause of most criminality. Fortunately, most human beings dispel aggression in socially acceptable ways. The sex offender does not. For inexplicable reasons, he is different. As a student of human nature and having interrogated thousands of criminal suspects, it's my opinion that the need for recognition is second only to aggression as a causative agent in criminality.

Murderers have told me, "I needed to get their respect." Armed robbers have told me, "It's a thrill to control somebody with a gun." Shoplifters have told me, "It's a high to beat the system." In sex crimes, the need for recognition is always a factor. The need for recognition is definitely tied to the sex drive. Whether it is the factor of territorial imperative or the subtlety of preening, the quest is to give the impression of being a desirable mating partner. The sex drive, primarily in criminal male offenders, appears to have an insatiable appetite. It's so consuming that many sexual offenders have told me that they had wished at times they had a frontal lobotomy operation. In most of the sexual offenders, there is a resignation that they just can't control themselves. The desire to commit the sexual act is consuming to them. Fantasizing the act and masturbation are insufficient to quench their desires. Eventually, the fantasizing had to be extended to a greater sexual sensation. The criminal sex offender constantly strives to make the overt act as great as the anticipation of it.

Other than aggression and the need for recognition, it has been my experience that child molesters have other things in common. Young victims represent virgin territory and that excites the molester's imagination and heightens the strength of the impulse to commit a sexual act. Child molesters are more comfortable with children than with people in their own age category. Psychologists say that pedophilia is a form of infantile regression. I've noted that child molesters appear to be hypersexual individuals, constantly preoccupied with sexual desires. Many of them are glib individuals who employ that ability to put their potential victims in a position to be seduced. Many are alcoholics, which adds to the problem of no self-control. Mostly, what they have in common is their ability to lie. Occasionally, an interrogator may be confronted with a suspect who is up in age but is not a true pedophiliac. This particular suspect has not spent his life molesting children. His sexual prowess has waned, and a child becomes an exciting and less threatening sex object to reach an erection, they satisfy their sexual urge by fondling the child. In most instances they are much easier to interrogate than a true pedophiliac because they have guilt feelings and possess a conscience, which is not characteristic of most child molesters.

In the confessions I have obtained from various sex offenders, most of them told me they fantasize the act before its commission. Recognizing that the need for recognition is a catalyst for most criminal behavior, I decided to use that need as a tool in interrogation. Showing insight and understanding has a mesmerizing effect on suspects, particularly in reference to sex crimes. When an interrogator attempts to understand motivation, and tries to get the suspect to understand himself, it's flattering to the ego of the suspect. It's a way for the interrogator to ingratiate himself with the suspect. The offender has a curious interest in the interrogator's analysis, because most of them have spent their lives trying to figure themselves out. In any interrogation there is a symbiotic relationship between the interrogator and the suspect. They are bound together in a common quest to understand the nature of the suspect and this interaction has an intoxicating effect on the suspect. In essence, the suspect loves the attention. He begins to feed on it. In his whole life, the suspect has never had the degree of attention and recognition created in a professional interrogation session.

I learned the power of the *captive audience syndrome* many years ago. As already stated, jailers would frequently call stating that a suspect wanted to talk to me again and would not waste my time. Having failed to obtain a confession in the first interrogation session, I could not understand why in the second session, the confession came in minutes. Simply put, the suspect missed the attention. He wanted to reestablish the recognition he gained in his relationship with the interrogator. There is a saying that you tell a good listener too much. That is particularly true in an interrogation session. I have seen many people confess to the act of murder just because the interrogator was a good listener.

PROBLEMS IN THE INTERROGATIONS
OF THE SEX OFFENDER

I have always found the true pedophiliac and the arsonist who commits arson to defraud, the most difficult people to interrogate. Pedophiliacs have the highest rate of recidivism among all criminal inmates. They are poor candidates for rehabilitation regardless of the type of psychiatric therapy. Thus, they possess a denial factor which negates any desire to tell the truth. I have stated many times in lectures, that if people lie to themselves, they are much more difficult to interrogate than those who lie to me.

The interrogation of any sexual offender has roadblocks not common to the interrogation of suspects in other types of crimes. First, the suspect finds the interrogation a degrading experience, particularly if he is accused of molesting a small child. He construes the accusation as an attack on his manliness. Some criminals take pride in a well-planned bank robbery or a cleverly devised act of fraud. There is nothing for the sexual offender to be proud of.

The second roadblock is the fact that the accusation automatically places him in a perceived subservient position to the interrogator. Even the worst among us has an ego. An interrogator has to be cognizant of that fact. The third major problem in the interrogation of the sex offender is the fact that, although the offender might have an inclination to confess, there is a reluctance to discuss the gory details of their act. The fourth roadblock that sometimes the offenders have, is a masochistic desire to hurt themselves. They will go so far to carry this out, they will even turn down a lesser penalty offered by the state in a plea bargain session.

A fourth factor that you have to contend with is that the sexual offender does not want to give the complainant the satisfaction of winning. This is particularly true when a complaint has been filed with the police by a wife or girlfriend regarding the subject's suspected abuse of their child. The suspect does not want to give the complainant the satisfaction of hearing him admit his guilt. You don't always know the underlying impasse that keeps the suspect from confessing. Thus, in the interrogation of the sexual offender, you have to cover the waterfront in the interrogation arguments.

VARIOUS SUGGESTED ARGUMENTS TO BE EMPLOYED IN SEX CRIMES

To counteract the suspect's feeling of being in a degrading or subservient position to the interrogator, I suggest that you should point out the prevalence of the act on a worldwide basis. To show objectivity, the interrogator should point out that some life forces are beyond a person's control, and that the interrogator understands that fact. The interrogator should point out that the interrogation is not an effort to put them down, and that the only thing the interrogator is interested in is their credibility.

Don't give the impression that you are some kind of prude when it comes to sexual activity. No one wants to believe that they are all bad in nature. The interrogator should find some redeeming feature in the suspect's existence, and acknowledge that fact. This is a means of ingratiating yourself with the suspect. Suspects don't confess to interrogators they don't respect. The interrogator has to give the impression that he is not in the business of condemnation but someone easy to talk to. Most pedophiliacs have undergone extensive psychiatric therapy with little or no effect. They believe that they are beyond cure. The interrogator should argue that there is no rehabilitation without acceptance of guilt. It should be pointed out to the suspect that his problem will plague him for the rest of his life, unless he has the fortitude to accept his guilt and tell the truth.

To counteract the problem of a suspect not wanting to confess the gory details of the crime, you should preempt that road block by Indicating that there's no desire to go into painful details. You just want the suspect to acknowledge the victim is telling the truth. Invariably, if the suspect does in fact acknowledge that the victim is telling the truth, they will then provide the details. It is the old story, "take the wall down one brick at a time."

I have heard many interrogators say, "All I want to hear from you is why you did it?" I don't suggest that tactic. For me, it creates an additional roadblock to obtaining the truth. Frequently, the suspect doesn't know why he committed the act himself. The suspect finds the motive too degrading to reveal. Experienced interrogators, to get around this problem will suggest a face-saving out. The interrogator should understand that even the worst criminal has to go on living with himself. Most people are image-makers and they will always cast themselves in the best light, criminals are no different.

Frequently, when testing an inmate in prison, inmates will state, "You know Mr. Holmes, there are a lot of bad people in here." Ironically, the statement is made by inmates who have committed an act more heinous than most of their fellow inmates. The astute interrogator believes that you have to leave the offender with some dignity. You can do this by pointing out that you don't condone what he did, but you have respect for the fact that he had the fortitude to tell the truth.

To reiterate, Freud said that many human beings have a death wish. From what I have observed of life, I agree. That wish sometimes leads to a masochistic personality structure. If the interrogator gets the impression that the suspect is attempting to cut off his nose to spite his face, and that attitude is blocking a potential confession, an effort has to be made to change the suspect's attitude.

The interrogator should point out to the suspect that how he thinks presently will not be how he thinks in six months or two years hence. The interrogator should further point out, that he should not allow his emotions to dictate his thought process. As an interrogator, I suggest that you tell the suspect what he is doing and that he should not allow his present attitude to dictate his future. The interrogator should point out how frequent inmates regret that they didn't tell the truth when they had the chance.

If there is an acrimonious relationship between the suspect and the complainant I want to reiterate that people who lie out of hate are more convincing than those who lie out of fear are. To counteract this problem, it should be pointed out to the suspect that he cannot win. By lying, he will give his adversary the satisfaction of seeing him get the maximum penalty. It is a truism that some offenders get more time for lying than for what they actually did.

Keeping in mind that most people confess because of the self-interest principle, and to ingratiate themselves with their accusers, the following interrogational arguments are suggested:

1. Point out that he has a right to be represented by an attorney, but attorneys can only ensure a fair trial, they can't destroy State's evidence.

2. Point out that this is the subject's last chance to control his own destiny, that if he doesn't tell the truth to you, he will be caught-up in the system and system will dictate what will happen to him. If there are any mitigating factors as to why he committed the act, such as alcohol or drugs, he should reveal the fact. If he did something, but not quite as bad as what the child described, in his own defense, he should tell what he actually did. It should be pointed out that if he tells the truth in your office, it will look like he is sincerely sorry for what occurred. If he waits for a plea bargaining arrangement, it will look like he is not sorry for what he has done but just trying to save time spent in prison.

3. An effective argument is to tell the subject that the act was based not on his character, but his personal problems and psychological needs. You should point out that many men hate what they do and hate themselves for lack of self-control. You allow the suspect to rationalize his behavior by indicating that in your opinion, he is a byproduct of his own life experience, which dictated the vengeful act in question.

4. "When you commit a wrongdoing, there are only three things that you can do, be sorry for what you did, tell the truth, and then forget it."

5. "You should think of your image. Liars incur hatred. Contrition and remorse creates forgiveness. You cannot afford to insult the intelligence of people nor can you look like you are sacrificing the child's reputation for your own social survival."

6. "Any coward can go off in a corner and lie. The real test of manliness is to stand up and admit when you are wrong and what you did. You have to show the fortitude and the courage to tell the truth even when it is embarrassing. Liars just don't have the mental toughness to tell the truth. I don't read you that way, if I did, I wouldn't be wasting my time talking to you."

7. "You don't measure a person by a singular act. You measure them by the totality of their existence and the direction they go in life after they have committed a wrong."

8. "You don't measure a person by what they sink to, but what they can rise to."

9. "Beside this problem you have, you don't appear to be a totally bad person. You have some attributes that are commendable. Don't negate your good attributes by being a liar."

10. "You have nothing in this life but self-respect. That is basically what life is all about. When you lose your self-respect, you are guilty of the worst crime of all—a wasted life. You can only regain self respect knowing that you were man enough to own up to what you did wrong. A man should never be ashamed to own up to the fact that he committed a wrong—his admission of wrongdoing simply means he is wiser at the moment of truth than when he was lying."

11. "Failure to repent of one's wrongdoing is worse that the act itself. The act is a momentary thing. The failure to repent and to confess is the perpetuation of a sin for life. There is no repentance in the grave."

12. Explain how the act imprisons oneself—Explain the comparison between mental imprisonment and physical imprisonment. "Only you can tear down the mental walls to freedom."

13. "When you betray a child's trust, you betray yourself. Your punishment is that child's hatred, which endures for a lifetime. An error in judgement doesn't become a permanent mistake until you refuse to correct it."

14. "You are the captain of your own ship. I can't dictate anything to you. I can only give you some food for thought. Right now, you are not thinking rationally, you are thinking out of fear. Any decision about telling the truth has to come from you. I don't win any victory—I get paid whether you tell the truth or lie."

15. "The whole purpose of life is to achieve the highest degree of civilized behavior. You slipped a little bit and now you have an opportunity to get back on the right path. You have an opportunity to finish the race of life with self-respect. You can't do that by living the rest of your life with a festering lie."

INCEST CASES

Incest has a profound effect on ostensibly good families. Those who commit an incestuous act, are not generally true pedophiliacs who hang around schoolyards looking for a victim. The father who commits an act of incest, in most instances is not predisposed to commit other criminal acts. Many are ashamed of what they did and seek forgiveness. Unfortunately, the act does irreparable harm to the victim, resulting in mental anguish that can last a lifetime. The mother of the victim is generally torn between an instinctive protective mechanism for her daughter and her effort to salvage her marriage. Everyone loses in these cases.

Incest is a historical and universal problem. For thousands of years, there were no sexual restrictions against adultery, incest or even bestiality. Ancient people knew the power of the sex impulse. The Jewish Talmud was the first written document that set forth prohibitions against having sex with children. Even today, many cultures do not put the emphasis on this type of behavior, in contrast to our society, with our puritan ethic background. To me, incest boils down to a convenient and accessible victim who becomes an insidious extension of the offender's desire to obtain absolute control.

During the interview of the incest suspect, the interrogator will observe certain defense mechanisms that are generally associated with guilt. Projection is one of these defense mechanisms. Projection is the tactic of thrusting ones guilt outwardly; specifically against the victim or in general terms, against the world. Examples of projection are revealed in the following remarks.

1. "Somebody put the idea in her head. She is just saying that because she was told to say that. They are using her.
2. "I heard she fools around. She even once came on to me."
3. "She has a reputation for telling stories."
4. "She is having trouble in school."
5. "She doesn't like being disciplined and she is getting even because I punished her."

The second defense mechanism that you see many times is disassociation. This is a thinking away process that reveals itself by general evasiveness. The defense mechanisms of disassociation are evident in responses to the following questions.

1. "Why is your daughter saying this about you?" Answer: "I don't know."
2. "Have you asked your daughter why she is saying this?" Answer: My lawyer told me not to discuss it with anybody."
3. "Have you asked your wife what this is all about?" Answer: "We really haven't discussed it. She just says that my daughter made the statement that I fool around with her."

Most people either justify an act at the time they do it or they seek a justification at a later time. In incest cases, the following remarks generally indicate the offender's attempt to justify the incestuous act.

1. "I treat her better than anybody else."
2. "She's always asking me for money."
3. "I'm the one who buys her nice things for Christmas and her birthdays."

THE INTERROGATION OF THE INCEST SUSPECT

The interrogator, in my opinion, should first suggest to the suspect a plausible explanation for why the offender came in contact with the child's private parts. The interrogator, to obtain a wedge, should suggest that things got out of hand in an innocent wrestling match, a bathing situation or the application of a medicinal salve to or near the child's private parts. The interrogator should point out that perhaps initially no wrongdoing was intended. If the suspect is not receptive to this approach, then a more forceful and assertive tactic has to be employed. Explain to the suspect that incest is an act that most societies sweep under the rug because there is a universal understanding of the difficulty of controlling the sex drive. The interrogator should point out to the suspect that what he has done is not a sign of insanity but an act committed by thousands in the evolutionary process. The argument has the value of diminishing the stigma of the act and gives the interrogator the appearance of being an understanding individual.

In the section describing the three major types of interrogational arguments, I cited the argument that has been successful for me in incest cases. For the purpose of continuity, in this section, I would like to repeat that argument.

> Let me tell you something that you don't understand. Your daughter's accusation against you is bad enough but what you are doing right now by denying the act is even worse. The mind of a child your daughter's age is like a piece of silly-putty. It can be shaped in any direction. Right now, she needs fortification and assurance that she did the right thing in telling her mother what you did. When a child is telling the truth and the adults are saying that she's lying she can get to the point where she doubts her own mind. She could easily splinter off from reality and in that sense, you could have done

irreparable harm to her by tearing her thought processes asunder. As men, we can't understand what these experiences mean to women or little girls. They can get over the uncomfortable feelings about the physical act, but what does the long-term emotional damage is the sense of betrayal and the loss of the ability to trust. It can keep a woman from being able to go on and have a happy marriage or be a good parent. I do not think your daughter hates you, but even at her age she knows what you were doing was wrong. She probably feels guilty about taking part in what happened but her greatest fear right now is of losing your love and approval. If you make her out to be a liar, you risk incurring her hatred for the rest of your life. I don't think you meant to harm her in these ways. She needs you to tell her that she did the right thing. You have the alternative of suffering the momentary embarrassment of relating to me what you did or carrying the weight of this guilt for the rest of your life for creating an unstable personality in your child. You can rectify a bad situation for both of you by telling the truth and start rebuilding your relationship with your child. I think you have to muster up the fortitude to tell the truth and bring stability to your daughter's life. Now she is telling the truth, isn't she?

RAPE CASES

If anything personifies human aggression gone awry, it is the crime of rape. In my opinion, every criminal who is not an overt homosexual is a potential rapist of women. If one possesses a predisposition toward criminality, they don't generally draw the line on rape. The rapists I have interrogated had several possible motives.

1. The control freak–This offender is aroused by the total subjugation of the victim.
2. The sadistic rapist–this offender likes to watch the victims suffer. Sadistic rapists just don't enjoy normal sex. Sexual pleasure comes only from inflicting pain.
3. The revenge rapist–This subject rapes to get even for a real or imagined grievance against a woman in his past.
4. The opportunistic rapist–This criminal takes advantage of a convenient victim while committing a burglary or armed robbery.
5. The justifying rapist–This offender has a hostility toward women and thinks they are asking for it.

6. The low-esteem rapist–This offender feels unappealing and unable to seduce women by verbal glibness. He believes that rape is the only way he can obtain sexual satisfaction.
7. The compensatory rapist–This offender enjoys the conquest. The rape builds his self-esteem.
8. The date rapist–This offender justifies his act on the basis that the victim put herself in a compromising position. He rationalizes his act by convincing himself that she led him on and teased him.
9. The hate-mother rapist – Many rapists have a disdain for women resulting from a poor mother image. This image is transmitted to all women and sometimes acts as a catalyst for the act of rape.

It should be pointed out to the suspect that there is just too much evidence against him to lie around. The interrogator should capitalize on the suspect's fear of the testimony of the victim. The suspect should be told that he can ill afford to go against the testimony of the victim in a court of law. If she sounds good and looks good in her testimony, the jury will believe her. You should point out to the suspect that a jury doesn't always know when someone is lying, but they have an instinct for knowing when someone is telling the truth. The suspect should be told if there is any mitigating factor in the case, it should be stated. Perhaps the victim exaggerated her testimony, maybe there was no penetration, which makes this an assault case rather than a rape case.

The interrogator has to cover a multitude of potential arguments, any one of which might induce a confession. For example, the interrogator can portray the victim as seductive by manner of speech and dress. That the victim triggered what occurred by permitting kissing and fondling, but didn't want to go further. It should be pointed out that if this was the case, it is understandable because men are not built like women. The interrogator can suggest that the victim may be screaming rape because, "You didn't give her the money you promised." It should be pointed out to the suspect that an illegal drug or alcohol caused him to commit an act he would not do under normal conditions. The interrogator could help the suspect project his guilt by suggesting that he was frustrated by a cold wife. All of these arguments are a means of achieving the ultimate goal of the interrogator, which is to get the suspect to admit at least contact with the victim.

In gang rape cases, the quest of the interrogator should be to get some participants in the rape to testify against the others. This is done by selecting the suspects most likely to confess as to what occurred. You should point out to the suspect that you are not making any promises but some people in this case are going to be witnesses and the others defendants. The interrogator should point out that perhaps rape was not his idea. That maybe he just assumed the victim was submitting voluntarily and that he didn't apply any force to have sex with her. The interrogator should point out to the suspect that the first guy who had sex with the victim was using him and the others to cover his crime. The interrogator should state: "You should have no reservations about testifying against your buddy because he initiated the rape and got everybody present arrested." The interrogator has done his job if the suspect admits contact with the victim. When the interrogator has eliminated the problem of identification, the testimony of a truthful victim is generally sufficient to convict.

INTERVIEWING THE RAPE VICTIM

In the 1950s and 1960s, there were complaints that policemen were not sympathetic enough with rape victims. Even worse was the complaint that some policemen had a vicarious interest in going over the gory details of the rape. These complaints led to the development of rape crisis centers where victims are medically examined and interviewed. I think the concept of rape crisis centers has merit.

While I was with the Miami Police Department, I interviewed and polygraph tested hundreds of rape victims. The interview of a rape victim has to be a delicate procedure. This is the one instance where the interrogator should play some role in the therapy administered to a truthful victim. Many victims of rape have guilt feelings because they are constantly asking themselves, "Did I resist enough." An interrogator has to be extremely careful not to invoke additional guilt by implying that perhaps the victims did not resist enough or did something stupid to place herself in jeopardy. The interrogator must give the impression that he is sympathetic and does not doubt the story of the victim. The interrogator should point out to the complainant that rape is a common offense and that she should be commended for coming forth and making the complaint. Rape victims need to express feelings and the interrogator should lend a sympathetic ear.

The questions should be done in a chronological form. This helps the victims recall the sequence of crucial events. The main thrust of the interview should be to determine the degree of force. Was it verbal or physical? What physical acts did the rapist actually do? As the interview progresses, the interrogator should make a subjective analysis as to whether the victim's emotions are genuine or appear contrived. One of the best barometers of truthfulness is the victim who appears to actually relive the experience as she relates it. Truthful subjects can answer any question posed by reasonable inquiry.

If the interview is done in a sympathetic and professional manner but the alleged victim is evasive and hostile, look out. If the alleged victim starts to personalize the interview by criticizing the questioner, look out. These are not good signs. If you observe evasiveness and hostility, the interrogator should then become more assertive in his questioning. The interrogator should make an effort to resolve contradictions in the alleged victim's story. The secret to good interviewing is to constantly force the storyteller to be more explicit. A fabricated story falls apart with in-depth questioning. The interrogator should evaluate as to whether the storyteller is relying on memory or making it up in an effort to respond to questions.

To reiterate, the interrogator should always start out giving the impression that he believes the victim until he sees signs that raise questions regarding the credibility of the storyteller. At that point, the interrogator should be more assertive.

REPORTED RAPE VICTIMS

When a rape victim suffers obvious physical injuries, there is generally little dispute among policemen that a rape actually occurred. When there are no obvious physical injuries, to some investigators the alleged victim's credibility is suspect. This is unfortunate because many women are raped without sustaining obvious physical injuries. In many cases, force is just implied either by verbal threats or the presence of a gun or knife. It's been my experience that in those instances when women do lie about rape, they do so for multiple reasons. Some lie because they were placed in an embarrassing situation wherein their contention of being raped is the only exculpatory explanation. They lie because they fear the reactions of a husband, boyfriend or family. Some lie for revenge against someone who has mistreated them.

Sometimes the victim is an agent of her own victimization. She may possess a tormentor type of personality with a basic hostility toward men. She may enjoy teasing more than the actual sexual act. Sometimes her behavior goes one bridge too far and incurs the wrath of the male who justifies using force to commit the sexual act.

During my career I have told several women, "You better get rid of that guy or he's going to kill you." One time I was right. I could never understand the masochistic nature of these women. With more experience, it became apparent to me that there is a sufferer's type of personality wherein the victim seeks self-punishment. In some rape cases, the victim who has this type of personality has a symbolic relationship between herself and her assailant. In her claim of rape, she represses her psychological needs that were a contributing factor in the act. You get the impression in talking to this type of personality that being abused is a pleasurable experience and therefore they place themselves consciously or otherwise in a self-defeating position.

INDECENT EXPOSURE

You will recall that in the beginning of my writing about sex crimes I stated that the need for recognition is a major factor underlying most sex crimes. The exhibitionist, or flasher, represents the need for recognition in its most twisted form. Most of the flashers I have interrogated have been white, young, in the building trades [I don't understand the significance of that] and at the time of the act their wives were pregnant. Many of the flashers when apprehended had their shirt off.

The act of exhibitionism is an enactment of fantasies. Those acts are generally followed by masturbation. The acts are a substitution for rape. The flasher is too fearful to commit the act of rape. To them, there is a sadistic delight in shocking their victims. The act reassures their masculinity. Those who make obscene telephone calls are committing acts of verbal exhibitionism.

INTERROGATION ARGUMENTS

As in all sex cases, your quest is to get the suspect to admit contact with the victim. Once he admits that, you can formulate all kinds of excuses for his behavior, but first you have to get the suspect to admit the possibility of exposure. You can offer the excuse that perhaps he was drunk or high on drugs. Maybe he just urinated and left himself exposed. The interrogator can suggest that he was having stomach problems and loosened his trousers resulting in his zipper being unfastened.

If the suspect seems receptive to any of these excuses, eventually you have to get around to the real reason for his act. The interrogator should point out that the suspect has a compulsion to commit these acts which are, in fact, aberrant self-expressions. If his behavior involves children, the interrogator should point out the high rate of recidivism among those who expose themselves. The suspect should be told if he can't control his sexual impulses, his behavior sets him up for a much more serious accusation such as having rape in mind. It should be further pointed out that if all he had in mind was to expose himself that he should state that, thereby avoiding the possibility that his behavior might be misconstrued. It should be noticed that most flashers are hypersexual in nature and they know that. The interrogator can employ empathy as a tactic by acknowledging the difficulty of controlling an irresistible impulse.

MISCARRIAGE OF JUSTICE CASES

In the 1950s and 1960s it was extremely rare that an alleged victim lied about being sexually abused. During those years, it was risky for a polygraph examiner to clear a suspect accused by a child of being molested. Then, things changed. Many young medical interns became self-professed experts in child sexual abuse cases and any injury to a child's private parts became absolute proof a child had been abused. The catalyst for this change was a book written about undetected sexual abuse of children and, in essence, the book blamed those in the medical profession for failing to detect indications of sexual abuse when children were examined. This contention led to paranoia in the medical profession and an overreaction. Subsequently, in my opinion many parents became unjustly accused of abusing their children. Commencing in the 1970s, there was a proliferation of accusations regarding sexual abuse of children. The increase in these cases was astronomical. What once used to be less than 5 percent of my testing workload, became 45 percent.

I often wondered if the notoriety given a particular criminal act, which makes the act appear commonplace, could in turn negate the stigma of the act which for years acted as a deterrence. One thing is for sure, either the crime of child sexual abuse has increased dramatically or the accusations have.

Compounding the problem are the so-called experts in the forensic field who specialize in child abuse cases. It's amazing to me how many assistant state attorneys accept the testimony of these so-called experts without question. For example, the testimony of child interview experts who utilize the anatomical doll to bolster their contention that a child was in fact molested. Even more suspect are memory retrieval experts who explore the deepest recesses of the mind and state without equivocation a particular client was molested twenty years ago. Adding to the problem, are overzealous social workers who believe that every accused is guilty because they fear a case may backfire on them.

Nationwide, there have been some terrible miscarriages of justice involving daycare operators caught up in the paranoid frenzy that many daycare operators have a propensity to abuse children. Miscarriage of justice cases do not occur in overwhelming numbers, but even one is too many. An astute interrogator has to act as a check and balance against the possibility of contrived testimony, which could lead to a miscarriage of justice case. I learned with experience that occasionally a vengeful wife during a divorce proceeding, and in an effort to obtain custody of her children, will use as the ultimate weapon the accusation her husband molested their daughter. In these cases, the child's testimony is rehearsed like a poem. In many cases the child's testimony is orchestrated by a hateful grandmother or other relative of the child. In retrospect, contrived testimony is rare but it does occur. A good interrogator can prevent a possible miscarriage of justice by taking nothing for granted and maintaining an objective viewpoint. Errors are made because some cases defy human analysis. In a troubling case, the interrogators should at least have the personal satisfaction of knowing they took everything into consideration.

Chapter VIII

MURDER CASES

THE INTERROGATION OF THE MURDER SUSPECT

We have over twenty-five thousand murders a year in the United States and one might get the impression that murderous aggression is infused in the marrow of our bones. Murder is universally considered to be the most heinous type of crime but despite that fact, murder suspects are not the most difficult subjects to interrogate. I often wondered about that and came to the conclusion that the taking of a human life has an effect on the perpetrator like no other crime. I also believe that even if they're not convinced there is a master painter, without a guarantee one way or the other, they're concerned about divine retribution.

The key to interrogation of murder suspects is understanding motivation for the act. Understanding motivation suggests the potential arguments or themes to be employed. I once read a quote by a Houston Medical Examiner who stated that most murders are caused by "babes, bucks and booze." I don't disagree with that, but I want to discuss additional causes of murder based on my life experience. Around 1955, I was the only polygraph examiner on the East Coast of Florida from Jacksonville to Key West. During those years I worked on as many as three or four murders a week. From those cases and the ones that followed in the years since, I want to outline different types of murder suspects and suggested interrogational arguments.

MURDERS COMMITTED BECAUSE OF
UNCONTROLLED RAGE

This is the number one reason for murders in our society. Uncontrolled rage causes murder in domestic disputes, neighborhood quarrels, fights in bars, card games, traffic disputes and child killings. All of these crimes have one thing in common; someone lost self-control. During the moments when self-control is lost, the consequences of the behavior are not considered. Rage bursts the dam of the inhibitory centers of the brain.

I learned from talking to many suspects that aggression is not static. It constantly builds up until it is dispelled; sometimes it is dispelled in a murderous impulse. An incident can cause aggression to be released in a murderous act or the aggressor will seek an excuse to release his pent-up emotions. This real or imagined grievance becomes the excuse for dispelling aggression. People vary in the amount of aggression they possess and their ability to manage anger. Generally, the killer in an uncontrolled rage murder has a lifelong history of temper displays.

INTERROGATIONAL APPROACH. With this type of suspect, you have one thing in your favor; his uncontrollable temper has been a lifelong problem and has caused most of the difficulties in his life. Suspects will acknowledge that fact and tell you that they sometimes hate themselves for their lack of self-control. As an interrogation technique, I like to project guilt onto the victim by indicating to the suspect that I don't think the crime was pre-meditated, but was triggered by the victim. I tell him that:

> What it boils down to is either the victim caused you to lose self-control or you are just evil, what impression do you want to give? Don't compound what you have done by being a liar. There is a mitigating factor here that people can understand. You just lost it. People can relate to that. You were not the captain of your ship during those moments of anger. I've talked to you long enough to know that you're no raving maniac. You certainly wouldn't have committed the act in the mental state that you are in right now. I don't think that an evil disposition caused this act. If you're going to be honest it was caused by your weakness in self-control. Now, you did kill him for that reason didn't you?

MURDERS COMMITTED TO ELIMINATE A WITNESS

In cases of armed robbery, rape or child molestation, the perpetrator kills to eliminate a witness. There are both practical and psychological reasons why these murders are committed. There is a basic philosophy among criminals, "Don't leave any witnesses." I once tested a young man accused of committing eight murders from Riverside, California to Miami, Florida. Over a period of two days of interrogation, he admitted committing the murders one by one. When he had finally gotten all of the murders off his chest, he told me that his older brother, also an armed robber, had told him "Never leave any witnesses."

There is also a psychological reason why murder is committed when it wasn't initially intended. Armed robbers, rapists and child molesters all enjoy the control and power they have over the victim. The victim's plight and pleading heighten the sensation of control. The ultimate control is to cause death. Once the sensation of control sets in, the murderer can't turn it off like a water faucet. The climax to the ultimate control is the act of murder.

INTERROGATIONAL APPROACH. In this type of case, the overall approach is to suggest to the suspect that murder was never intended, that the victim said or did something to cause his demise. Point out that, "You hate what you fear. The victim said or did something that made you fearful that you would be caught and convicted based on the victim's witness testimony. This engendered the emotion of hate and once that emotion was turned on you were unable to stop it. It was this hatred that triggered the murderous act."

MURDERS COMMITTED BECAUSE OF
AMBIVALENT FEELINGS

Mixed feelings can lead to frustration and stress and stress can lead to violence. The act of murder is a last ditch effort to maintain one's sanity. I once tested a young man who spent his life taking care of his elderly parents. One night they berated him for the way he cooked their pork chops. He picked up a frying pan and bludgeoned them to death.

I had this same situation with an engineer who took care of his invalid wife. She was constantly complaining to the point where it was affecting his work performance. One morning, totally frustrated by her incessant complaints, he put a pillow over her face and smothered her to death. He told me that while he was smothering her, he had such difficulty accepting what he was doing, that he felt like he was standing outside his own body watching himself commit the act. This is a statement I've heard many times from those who have committed the act of murder.

After this type of killing there is a high degree of anguish because the perpetrator realizes that he has killed somebody he loved. After the murder is committed, he reflects back and questions whether the situation was so bad that it had to be resolved by murder. The perpetrator tries to rationalize his act, but that mental process is undermined by the memory of the good times he enjoyed with the victim.

INTERROGATIONAL APPROACH. In this type of murder, the interrogator should describe how ambivalent feelings lead to a love-hate relationship. He should point out to the suspect that the victim was in essence, "driving him nuts," and that when he thought he was about to lose his mind he lost all self-control and committed an act which totally belies his basic good character. Explain that the murder was committed because of the cumulative effect of being tossed between feelings of love and agony. With the use of empathy and sympathy, the interrogator can usually get these suspects to confess.

MURDERS COMMITTED FOR REVENGE

I've always been fascinated by how far people will go to get revenge. From what I've seen, I'm convinced that revenge is instinctive and plays a definite role in the evolutionary process. A culture is in jeopardy of extinction if it is not capable of giving its predators the message that they will pay the price for committing untoward acts. But revenge is a double-edged sword in that it causes cultural problems and is viewed as atavistic. That belief is probably the basis for the biblical quote, "Vengeance is mine sayeth the Lord." The need for revenge is like a burning ember. Some people would rather die than not achieve revenge. They are not deterred by the potential consequences of their act.

I once tested a deputy sheriff who got in a fight in a bar and was severely beaten. He went outside to his truck and waited for his assailants to emerge. When they came out of the bar, he shot them down with a high-powered rifle. He initially admitted being in a fight with them but denied the killings. He claimed that he had driven away after leaving the bar. Based on a description of his truck he was stopped by the police several hours later. He was brought to me for polygraph testing. When I pointed out to him that it was obvious to me that he had too much pride to take an ass whipping without retaliation, I got his attention. I told him that when he got into his truck he made the decision that he couldn't live with himself unless he did something regardless of the consequences. He nodded in agreement and confessed.

It should be noted that those who lie to cover an act of revenge are more convincing that those who lie out of fear. They feel justified both in the act and in their lies. In most instances, they have no guilt feelings; on the contrary, they have an air of satisfaction. Revenge murders are sometimes viewed as a "badge of honor." The act enables the perpetrator to regain his self-respect and increases his manliness. The tremendous increase in the number of fired or disciplined employees without criminal records who kill their bosses clearly indicates the universal nature of revenge.

INTERROGATIONAL APPROACH. Because the perpetrator feels justified in his act, these are difficult suspects to interrogate. Women are much easier to interrogate than men in these cases because, in most instances, they have been abused and it's readily apparent why they committed the act of murder. By commiserating with the female suspect, the interrogator can obtain a confession that might not be forthcoming from a male suspect.

With the male suspect, I generally argue that the victim was an agent of his own victimization and the catalyst for the act. I point out that in view of the amount of evidence against the suspect, that his lying will secure the conviction and maximum penalty, thus giving the victim the final revenge. I argue that if he felt justified in doing the act, and there was a mitigating factor, that he should state that now.

MURDERS THAT LOOK LIKE ACCIDENTS

There are a lot of sadistic people who have a fascination with death who create scenarios where they know death could occur but which would allow them to later claim it was an accident. I've seen this in boating "accidents," "accidental" discharges of guns and "games" that cause death. The people who cause the death get away with murder because there is no ostensible motive. Actually, the motive is their sadistic nature. They enjoy tempting fate. Someone who cannot swim or someone terrified of guns becomes the foil in a sadistic game that results in his death. The victim's fear makes it even more exciting for the sadist.

I've been frustrated in my career by people who I knew deliberately overturned a boat knowing their companion couldn't swim or deliberately discharged a firearm and pretended it was an accident. Because murder couldn't be proven, the only satisfaction I had was telling them in no uncertain terms that I knew what they had done. You will generally find that the people responsible for these "accidents" have a history of playing sadistic games. They are always doing things to place people in jeopardy so they can see their fear.

INTERROGATIONAL APPROACH. Generally, the only way you can differentiate between deliberate acts and accidents and resolve these cases is with the polygraph. These people always have ready and exculpatory excuses. They know deep down what they did, but they always rationalize that it was an accident. In most instances, the polygraph test results are the only interrogational argument you have to get the suspect to admit he committed a deliberate act.

I would like to make the distinction between two types of individuals who commit murders that look like accidents. First, those who by their nature like to play sadistic games with anybody and secondly, the individual who sets up a specific scenario to cause a specific death which he later claims was an accident. Too often I've heard this story from the latter. "We were just playing a game. I was throwing the baby up in the air and then catching him. I don't know what happened, but he slipped out of my hands and fell on his head." As you investigate this type of case, you will find that the perpetrator felt that the baby was an irritant in his relationship with the mother. The baby's incessant crying became the final straw that caused his resentment to culminate in murder. The interrogational approach I would take with this suspect would be to point out that the baby's aggravating crying put him in a state of mind to subconsciously desire the baby's death.

MURDERS COMMITTED BY THE SEXUAL PSYCHOPATH

Most serial killers are sexual psychopaths. There is a degree of aggression in every sexual act that guarantees the perpetuation of the species. With the sexual psychopath, there is a pathological increase in the degree of aggression. For the sexual psychopath there is no sexual satisfaction without the aspect of sadism. We can leave the job of compiling the psychological profile and defining causality to the academics, but as an interrogator there are some things that you have to know. To help you identify these subjects review the discussion of the sociopath and psychopath in "How People Lie."

INTERROGATIONAL APPROACH. With the sexual psychopath it's extremely difficult for the interrogator to reconcile the acts committed with the suspect he's talking to. Sexual psychopaths do not have fangs and they are not foaming at the mouth during the interrogation. Most of the time they look like choirboys. They have a facade of normality that allows them to operate in society without being detected. It's rare that you can get a sexual psychopath to talk about what he did and why. Over the years, I've worked on several cases where the suspect was a sexual psychopath. Because of their makeup and the abhorrent nature of their acts, you rarely get a frank disclosure. Once in a while you luck out.

I worked on a case in Massachusetts with Polygraph Examiner Charles Zimmerman. The suspect had killed several women and dismembered their bodies. The suspect was highly articulate and well-read. Over a period of several hours, we used a conditioning process where we got him to talk about the case hypothetically. Understanding that he was "only talking about the murders hypothetically" he became so excited sharing his ideas that he slipped into a first person relation of what had occurred. He took a sadistic delight in watching our reaction to his vivid descriptions of the killings.

This type of interrogation can be more draining on the interrogator than on the suspect. With the sexual psychopath, the formula needed to induce a confession is the use of the three Ps, persistence, persever-

ance and patience. An overall approach, I've had some measure of
success with in interrogating the sexual psychopath is to show an
intense fascination with the suspect. This plays to his conceit. He may
then fall victim to the axiom, "You tend to tell a good listener too
much."

MURDERS COMMITTED BECAUSE OF GREED

I have already discussed the inherently acquisitive nature of
mankind. In murders committed because of greed this characteristic
is obsessional. Material things are a status symbol. Their possession
gives the individual recognition which, in my opinion, is the most
powerful motivating force in life aside from the law of self-preserva-
tion. Greed murders occur among business partners, in insurance
fraud, and in inheritance disputes. The drug culture provokes many
murders arising out of territorial disputes, drug rip-offs, etc.

INTERROGATIONAL APPROACH. These are tough cases because
you're dealing with people who had given a lot of thought as to how
to commit the act and get away with it. You don't get a confession in
these cases as a rule unless you have an overwhelming amount of evidence that they can't lie around. These suspects don't confess because
of a stricken conscience. They are generally glib and good at con-
structing plausible stories.

In this type of case, when a confession is not forthcoming, and the
defendant is prosecuted based on circumstantial evidence, a single
major discrepancy in the suspect's story to the police can be a decid-
ing factor in obtaining a conviction. The discrepancy could be in the
suspect's alibi or statements he made regarding his relationship to the
victim, finances or post-act behavior. But that discrepancy has to be
well-documented by tape recording or in written form. There should
be no doubt in a jury's mind as to what the suspect told the police in
his defense. A good interrogator can sense key remarks made by a
suspect that could become a vital issue in court, even if the suspect
never confessed. The documentation should be irrefutable, so that in
court, the defendant can't say, "I never told the police that." Too
many times, notations are not made of a suspect's remarks which
become vital issues in a court trial.

MURDERS COMMITTED OUT OF JEALOUSY

Almost every troublesome emotion in life is a necessary ingredient in the evolutionary process. I'm particularly referring to aggression, revenge and jealousy. I suspect that jealousy plays a role in natural selection and is a propelling force for achievement. Jealousy is a resentment arising out of any competitive situation. It's triggered by fear of loss or rejection, and rejection is withdrawn recognition. Those two factors cause murder. More than once during a confession to a murder committed because of jealousy I've heard, "If I can't have her no one's going to have her." The murder gives the killer possession and control into perpetuity. The hatred is compounded if the rejection is viewed as unjust. The murder is committed when the jealousy builds up to a crescendo and revenge takes over.

INTERROGATIONAL ARGUMENT. In this type of murder I point out to the suspect that what he did is a very common act on this planet because no one has control over the emotion of jealousy. I explain that in some sense jealousy is an expression of love. Once this emotion sets in, no rational thought process can deter such a strong emotion. If the interrogator finds out that the victim did something to trigger the emotion of jealousy then he should project guilt onto the victim, thus giving the perpetrator a face-saving out. This type of suspect is highly susceptible to any type of argument that indicates his act was understandable. The interrogator should state that throughout history thousands of people have committed the same act. This argument minimizes the seriousness of the crime making it easier to obtain a confession.

MURDERS COMMITTED BECAUSE OF A
PASSIVE AGGRESSIVE PERSONALITY

After a crime you often hear the remark, "I can't believe he did it, he's so quiet." The passive aggressive who commits murder has allowed hostility to build up over a lifetime. Every time he has been humiliated, he has retained the grievance in his memory bank. At the time of the alleged injustice, he does not seek revenge because he is afraid of the consequences. He satisfies his need for revenge somewhat by fantasizing about how he would have gotten even. Suddenly an incident occurs of sufficient provocation that causes an explosive release of suppressed hostility. He has been kicked in the face one too many times. His hostility climaxes in the act of murder.

The passive aggressive murderer may have a history of committing substitute acts to dispel hostility. He may be a gun collector who shoots at light poles and domestic animals. Closely akin to the passive aggressive murderer is the little weakling who tries to prove to his peers how tough he is by committing murder. The killing is a means of showing up his companions. He commits the act as a compensatory mechanism for his low status among his peers and hopes that it will raise his stature in the group. In the investigation of crimes with multiple suspects, it is often assumed that the one with the worst record did the actual shooting. However, often the suspect you would least expect turns out to be the one who did it.

INTERROGATIONAL APPROACH. When I have a suspect who is either a passive aggressive murderer or one who committed murder as a compensatory act I like to try to portray life in the worst light. I point out the injustices in life and how they can affect an individual's thinking. I try to create the feeling that life's injustices were a catalyst for the act committed. This type of suspect is susceptible to any interrogational argument that shows an understanding of his reasons for committing the act.

Blaming the world allows the suspect to project his guilt outwardly. The interrogator sets the stage by allowing the suspect to express his complaints thereby easing him into a full confession.

FALSE CONFESSIONS IN MURDER CASES

In my career, I have been involved in several cases where the validity of a confession made in a murder case became an issue. False confessions do occur in murder cases for the following reasons:

1. The publicity seeker–Mentally unstable people confess to the act of murder for attention and notoriety. Generally, they are masochistic in personality makeup and seek to find something tangible in reality to which they can attach their free-floating anxieties. Fortunately for an interrogator, their confessions are so bizarre in nature it is obvious that what they said emanated from a disintegrated thought process.

2. Guilt by omission rather than commission. Occasionally you will have a distraught husband state, "You might as well lock me up. I'm the murderer." They seek to punish themselves and to assuage guilt feelings for failure to prevent their wives' deaths. A security guard confessed to me he killed his daughter, when it was obvious she committed suicide with his gun and he was not around at the time she shot herself. He just couldn't handle being an indirect agent of her death.

3. "I am number one." Many multiple killers exaggerate the number of people they have killed to gain a reputation as the most prolific murderer in history. They enjoy being interviewed by police from all over the country who have unsolved cases they hope to resolve. They enjoy duping the police, which gives them a sadistic feeling of superiority. They enjoy the special attention they get at the hands of wishful investigators. Emmit Monroe Spencer confessed to me to killing 47 people. Actually, he killed four people. It took me a long time to differentiate the truth from fantasy.

4. False confessions that stem from physical and/or psychological abuse. As a polygraph examiner, these are the tough cases. Those who confess falsely generally fit the same profile. They are convenient suspects who were in the wrong place at the wrong time. They possess a low IQ. They are vulnerable to persuasive arguments.

Some are heavy drinkers and drug users. They falsely confess for the following reasons:

a. To get the police off their back because they just can't take any more physical or psychological abuse.

b. They assume that, at a later date, they can explain to their family or an Attorney why they falsely confessed.

c. They begin to doubt their own mind when told by police there is evidence against them or they lied during a polygraph examination.

d. They think that despite their innocence, they might be found guilty. They therefore become vulnerable to false promises that will save their life or result in less punishment.

e. They become intoxicated with the police attention and will say anything not to make the police angry and destroy a newfound relationship.

WHAT THE PROFESSIONAL INTERROGATOR HAS TO KNOW TO PREVENT MISCARRIAGES OF JUSTICE

1. You have to fight a natural tendency to believe a confession, even when you have serious doubts as to its validity.

2. You can't use yourself as a yardstick by assuming, "I wouldn't confess to a crime I didn't do." Note, the same yardstick has been used by many jurors who are misled by a false confession.

3. You have to remain objective and not be influenced by fellow investigators who have a vested interest in the case, and want to believe the confession obtained.

4. You may have doubts about the subject's guilt or innocence; however, sometimes the subject's testimony that he was beaten is so descriptive in nature, you cannot discount abuse as the underlying cause for making the confession.

5. You have to ask yourself, "How did the confession come about?," "Over what time period?," "What is the general reputation of the Interrogator who obtained the initial confession?," "Does he have a reputation for being overly intimidating and prone to making false promises?"

6. Did the confessor state in his confession anything that wasn't already known?

7. Did the confessor recite details that he might have picked up during the interrogation process?

8. Was there any conflict between what the confessor stated and the crime scene analysis?

9. Did the confessor supply any confirmation: murder weapon, fruits of the crime, documentation, witness, etc? Is there anything that links the confessor to the crime other than his word?

10. Did the confessor provide incidental details which lent credibility to his confession? Does the confession sound like a rehearsed poem?

11. Did the confessor provide quotations or remarks made by the victims or co-defendants?

12. Did the confessor answer all the questions that the actual perpetrator should be able to answer?

13. Did the confessor express genuine feelings of remorse and appear to be relieved?

Chapter IX

ESPIONAGE CASES

THE INTERROGATION OF SPIES, HATE GROUP MEMBERS AND ASSASSINS

In 1963, I left the Miami Police Department to open my own business. When I did that, I entered a new world of interrogational challenges. While on the police department I got used to interrogating murderers, rapists, armed robbers, burglars, etc. As a private polygraph examiner working for different government agencies and private attorneys, I began interrogating people accused of federal crimes. I administered polygraph examinations in the assassination of John F. Kennedy, and the murder of Dr. Martin Luther King. For the first time I was confronted with the task of interrogating people accused of conspiracy to commit assassinations, acts of espionage and bombings committed by hate groups. This was a different ballgame because the suspects thought what they did was noble and I was faced with the ideological beliefs they used as justification for their acts.

There have been volumes of material written by academics regarding the personality structure of individuals involved in assassinations and espionage. As an interrogator and polygraph examiner my primary concern was to determine guilt or innocence and not to fathom the nuances of complex personality structures. I did, however, learn empirically some basic principles underlying the personality make-up of the assassin and spy.

When the first entity crawled out of the primordial sea laying a foundation for human evolution, we became impaled on the horns of a perennial dilemma. The problem began when aggression became the fuel for the evolutionary process. Granted, there had to be a propelling force for evolution but aggression has been the bane of our existence in that it has caused wars, murders, and mayhem. I am convinced that the need to dispel aggression causes strife between different nations, races, and religions as well as different classes of people. In my opinion if there were no differences man would create a difference just to dispel aggression.

Assassins and hate group members adopt an ideology which is nothing more than a facade to lend justification to their criminal acts. Coupled with a need to dispel aggression is an almost obsessive desire for recognition. Assassins make the decision to gain immortality through the fame of committing a notorious act and despite what conspiracy buffs think, assassins don't want to share that immortality with anyone else. They are mentally well-prepared to accept the consequences of their act rather than be a nobody for the rest of their lives.

I tested a man who was a member of a hate group involved in bombing synagogues in the South and the bombing of the home of an editor of the Miami Herald newspaper. I learned through that experience the futility of engaging in an ideological debate. These people have such fixed beliefs to justify their behavior that they become very articulate in the presentation of their case. You can't win these debates because even if there might be some intellectual acceptance of what you say, there is no emotional acceptance. Their strident beliefs are just a vehicle for the release of aggression.

Occasionally, with spies you are forced into a position where you have to undermine the suspect's thinking. I have developed some arguments to be used in the interrogation of spies.

"Wrong Allegiance" Argument

This is a heterogeneous nation comprised of many different ethnic groups. Because of this fact, we have the problem of ethnocentrism, a belief in the inherent superiority of one's own group and culture. In my opinion, this is instinctive in nature. Some argue that allegiance to one's country of origin never dies. Foreign countries soliciting spies obviously work on that basic premise.

If an interrogator has the task of interrogating someone who is a resident or citizen of the United States but who is of foreign nationality then he must have the arguments to counterattack the suspect's justification that the espionage act was based on allegiance to a particular national heritage. The debate becomes very clear: Allegiance to the United States versus allegiance to the other nationality. Fortunately, the United States is an easy country to defend in any debate. America is not just a nation, it's the worldwide symbol for what's right for all mankind: individual freedom. Therefore, the interrogator should be able to argue convincingly that the espionage act was based on misguided allegiance. To be effective with this argument the interrogator should possess some knowledge of the history of the suspect's country. Whatever theme the interrogator employs must be factual and must impress the suspect with the objectivity of the interrogator's analysis. In a case in which someone of Polish descent was suspected of an act of espionage I developed the following interrogational argument:

> Mr. ____, in this case your guilt has been clearly established. Apparently, you've decided to lie about it because you feel justified in what you did and now you're prepared to be a martyr to protect Polish interests. I can understand that because we have the same problem with other nationalities. But your behavior is not easily understood. Evidently, you came to this country to enjoy our way of life. From what I understand you've done well for yourself and have been enjoying the fruits of our society. But, the first time someone tugged on your umbilical cord you decided to bite the hand that has been feeding you. You had a choice between hurting your new country or supposedly helping Poland. You probably assumed that by helping Poland you were helping the Polish people. Now let's examine that assumption.

> There are thirty-six million people in Poland and approximately two million are members of the Communist Party. Of those two million there are approximately one hundred thousand career bureaucrats who run the nation of Poland. The person who contacted you and seduced you into spying represents that elite corps of bureaucrats which is governed by a politburo which is under Russian control. Regardless of what you think, what you did was for the benefit of Russia and not Poland.

> In that sense, you were duped. The man that contacted you was actually being used by the Russians to solicit you as a spy. For strategic and geographic reasons, Poland is a satellite of Russian Imperialism. Now if that doesn't bother you it should. For thousands of years, yours has been a country of unrest. Primarily because at different periods of time it has been partitioned by either the Germans or the Russians. Poland has never enjoyed, for any reasonable peri-

od, a national sovereignty that was not jeopardized by predators from the East or West.

When Warsaw was being ransacked by the Germans the Russian army stood outside and watched while millions of innocent Poles were being killed. In 1944, when the Germans were pushed out of Poland, Russia placed thousands of Polish people in boxcars and shipped them to Siberia. If you had an election tomorrow in Poland less than ten percent of the Polish people would vote for the Communist Party. The Communists are in power in Poland for only one reason, and that is the presence of the Red Army. Those people who are members of the Communist Party in Poland are not members because they believe in ideology, they are members because it insures a bureaucratic and an elitist position in Poland.

Poland has had thirty-seven years of Communist rule and yet an unemployed worker on welfare in England makes more money than a Polish coalworker does as the top salaried employee in Poland. Now I don't know if you're a Communist or what you're political inclinations are, but I'm trying to understand your act in light of all that I have told you which are irrefutable facts.

Now let's examine the relationship between Poland and the United States. In 1791, Poland had the first constitution in Europe. It was a copy of the United States Constitution. At the YALTA Conference, the United States insisted that Poland be a sovereign nation. We insisted on free elections but because of the presence of the Red Army the election was rigged and the Communist Party came into power. Despite that fact and despite the fact that Poland is a satellite of Russia, the United States has loaned more money to Poland for development than all other countries combined. The United States has never been a threat to Poland in our entire history.

I want you to think just a moment and reflect on what I have said. Then ask yourself whether or not you made a mistake in committing an act which in the final analysis will not help the Polish people but will help a nation that has oppressed and slaughtered Polish people numerous times throughout history. The only way you can rectify the wrong that you have done to this country is to tell the truth and I want you to do that right now.

I want to reiterate that most people don't confess because of questions asked, but they do confess because of themes used. You have to sell someone on the concept of telling the truth.

"Traitor to Your Group" Argument

It is my opinion that if a person voluntarily becomes a spy he does so for two reasons: greed and rejection. If he is solicited by a foreign power and agrees to become a spy he also does it for two reasons: Greed and recognition. Man is instinctively acquisitive in nature, which means that he has the desire to acquire. This basic instinct probably developed through the evolutionary process, because man's survival during the winter months depended upon his ability to acquire and hoard sufficient food. Over time this instinct evolved into what we know today as a materialistic nature.

The voluntary spy justifies his act with a real or imagined grievance. Most of the time, as a result of not attaining the respect he desires, rejection becomes a powerful motivating force toward committing the act of espionage. His basic acquisitive nature adds to the decision to voluntarily spy. Those who have been solicited by a foreign power to spy do so because they have been seduced by recognition. Agents of foreign powers know how susceptible human beings are to attention. This factor is best described in the words of a song, "When I'm not near the one I love, I love the one I'm near." Foreign agents employ incessant flattery to create a camaraderie between themselves and the person being solicited. The foreign agent compromises the individual to a point where greed takes over.

A strange phenomenon takes place in the mind of the target. He knows he is entering into a compromising position but enjoys the attention and the flattery. He thinks he has control of the situation and can always bring it to a screeching halt. But most of the time, he ends up going one bridge too far. If personal attention by a foreign agent seduced the individual to commit an act of espionage, it just makes sense to me to use the same weapon to obtain the truth. The interrogator creates an intimacy between himself and the suspect through empathy. The interrogator helps the suspect justify his act by pointing out that it was his personal problems rather than a character defect that prompted the crime. Suspects feed on understanding and it they get it from an interrogator it creates a chemistry conducive to truth-telling. If commiserating with the suspect doesn't work then you have to shift gears to different interrogational approaches.

One approach is to invoke the emotions of guilt and shame in the suspect. You do that with the following argument:

In all human beings there is a need to belong, there is a need to identify with a particular group or segment. By belonging to a particular
group the members gain mutual recognition, love and security. This
in turn enhances social survival. Most people wouldn't chance the
loss of group respect but you took that step when you stole the documents and sold them to the Russians. You did that because of a base
human instinct: Greed. When you go against your own group, you
violate mutual trust. In essence, you are saying, 'I no longer identify
with you or need you.' By doing what you have done, you brought
upon yourself a shame that will endure until your last breath.

By your act you label yourself a traitor, one who will not be accepted by anyone else in the world community including the recipients
of the documents you stole. If you choose to lie about what you did,
you will flounder for the rest of your life in a sense of nonacceptance.
Only by telling the truth may you gain a measure of human dignity.
Only by telling the truth may you restore some degree of self-respect.
Only by telling the truth do you open the door to a potential restoration of public respect and acceptance. Why be a liar on top of what
you already did?

When you interrogate someone who is a member of a hate group,
you will find that these people are arrogant and disputatious in nature.
These people are usually glib without wisdom. To have any chance of
making them susceptible to interrogational arguments you have to
undermine their confidence that they did the right thing by joining the
hate group. I have used what I call "The Wasted Life" argument during interrogations of bombing suspects.

"Wasted Life" Argument

I get the impression in talking to you that you're an angry person. If
there were no Jews or blacks in the world, you'd find someone else
to hate. When you joined this group, you made an emotional decision, not a rational one. You were just looking for some way to vent
your spleen. When you made a decision to get involved in these
bombings, you also made a decision for your wife and children. You
are definitely going to go to prison, but, ironically, you're going to
suffer less agony than your family. Even though they will be free,
you've destroyed their spirit to live. By denying the crime, you are
sadistically tormenting your own family by giving the impression that
you're unjustly accused. Naturally, they identify with you, therefore,

you place them in an adversarial position toward their government. By doing this, you're poisoning the whole well. By telling the truth, you can teach your children to respect their institutions.

What you did is bad enough, but you committed the worst crime of all, a wasted life. You think that your ideas should be a yardstick for the whole world, but you nor anybody else is going to change the infinite scheme of things. There are certain life forces that nobody has control over. So, what you have been involved in, is an exercise in futility. No one can guarantee a permanent ideal system for governing human beings. Everything is cyclic in nature. One guy gets an idea, and you call that a thesis. Then, someone offers a contrary idea, and that's called an antithesis. Then a third guy comes along, and says, "Let's put the two ideas together," and they call that a synthesis. That cycle goes on to perpetuity. That has been true throughout recorded history. All of what you did isn't going to change a thing. How you think now may not be the way you think down the road. What you believe in now, you could very well abhor in later years.

Again, the crime you're guilty of is a wasted life. If you're going to be honest with yourself despite all your mental gymnastics, you know deep down that what you did was not worth the consequences of your act. You can try lying to yourself every waking moment, but there are periodic moments of reflection when you realize that what you did was a foolish thing. Now, the only way that you can rectify your behavior is by telling the truth. A failure to repent and confess, is a perpetuation of a sin for life.

A man should never be ashamed to own up to the fact that he has been wrong. Your admittance of wrongdoing will simply mean that you're going to walk out of this room a lot smarter than when you came in. Now, you were one of the guys that put the bomb in the synagogue, weren't you?

Assassins' Arguments

I've tested suspects who were accused of being co-conspirators in assassinations but I've never tested the actual shooter. I guess if I were confronted with the actual assassin I would approach him as I would any other murder suspect. There is, however, one major difference between the assassin and other murderers in that he committed the crime to gain immortality. He glorifies the act of murder. Since the act puts him on stage I think that the interrogator could argue that if he felt justified in committing the act then he (the suspect) should feel justified in telling the world what he did and why.

Since the assassin is enslaved by an obsessive need for recognition, that could be his Achilles Heel in an interrogation session. The interrogator could massage his ego to a point where the assassin would want to brag about what he did. At some point in the interrogation, I would use one of my favorite statements: " I have an academic interest in you." This gives the suspect the impression that he is something special as distinguished from the run-of-the-mill suspect. It's a technique for the interrogator to use to ingratiate himself and to give the suspect the impression, "You will never find a better listener than I am." In addition to this approach, I would use the traditional themes and arguments already outlined in the section pertaining to interrogation of the murder suspect.

Chapter X

MISCELLANEOUS CRIMES

ARMED ROBBERY CASES

The personality structure of the armed robber is different from that
of other criminals. He is more aggressive and prepared to kill.
For him, aside from the monetary reward of the act there is the thrill
aspect of committing armed robberies. Armed robbers enjoy the control they have over the victim. To have a victim in a pleading, cower-
ing position, afraid for his life, heightens the sadistic pleasure of the
robber. I've had many armed robbers tell me they get a high committing armed robberies. They are like mountain climbers, they enjoy
the excitement of putting their own life in jeopardy.

In most instances, it's extremely difficult to get a confession from an
armed robber unless the evidence is so strong they can't lie around it.
The penalty for armed robbery in most states is so severe it deters suspects from confessing. They live in hope that somehow they can beat
the rap. There is an approach that sometimes works when the suspect
is debating whether or not to confess.

The first thing that I do is to point out the incriminating evidence
against the suspect. Then I tell him, that he was actually lucky to be
caught, because it is the inevitable fate of most armed robbers that
they will have to kill or be killed. This observation heightens the fear
that most armed robbers have. The interrogator should then point out
that no matter how many armed robberies the suspect commits his
average take will be less than a hundred dollars and that statistically
most armed robbers are caught within a period of eighteen months.
Remind him that no matter how well the robber prepares to commit
the hold-up "the fluke" always gets them; whether it's the little old lady

the robber trips over while attempting to make his escape or the bad luck of being apprehended by an off-duty policeman who just happens to be in the store at the time the crime is committed. If "the fluke" doesn't get an armed robber he'll be identified by a fellow armed robber trying to make a deal to get out of a charge.

The interrogator should point out to the armed robbery suspect that, although he thinks he has control of his own behavior at the scene of a crime, he can't always control a trigger-happy partner. If his partner kills, both are charged with first-degree murder. Use these facts to create the picture that the armed robber is in a losing business, and that he is at the crossroad of his life. He can tell the truth about what he did and get out of the armed robbery business or suffer the eventual consequences of killing or being killed.

The interrogator should acknowledge that if the suspect confesses it will be used against him in this particular case but that same confession will save his life. State that this is the last time he has control of his destiny. Making the wrong decision locks him into a dire fate. This interrogational approach doesn't always work, but I've used it successfully enough times to justify its use when confronted with any armed robbery suspect.

As a polygraph examiner, you should be aware that many armed robbers have been involved in unsolved murders or they know about one. For that reason regardless of what testing technique you use, after you have concluded your examination of him in reference to the case in question, I suggest that you run one more test asking the armed robbery suspect, "Do you have knowledge of any unsolved murders?" If you get a deceptive response to that question you can shift into specific arguments employed in murder cases. We have over six thousand unsolved murders per year in the United States. A lot of these are committed during armed robberies. In my career, I have solved over ten murders by asking that question.

ARSON CASES

Over the years, as a police and private polygraph examiner, I've tested many arson suspects. They fall into two different categories, the emotional and nonemotional offenders.

The emotional offenders are susceptible to standard interrogational arguments. The nonemotional, those who set fires to defraud insurance companies, are one of the most difficult of all criminal suspects to interrogate. I'll explain why after first discussing the emotional offender. They include:

1. Those who set fires for sexual gratification.
2. Victims of rejection in lover's quarrels who set fires out of revenge.
3. Disgruntled employees who have a real or imagined grievance against their employer and set their employer's business on fire.
4. Those who set fires to cover a crime such as murder.
5. Those who set fires to become a hero by discovering the fire, such as volunteer firemen, guards and various hotel employees.
6. Children who set fires out of anger or fascination with fire.

The key to interrogating the emotional fire-setter is to show insight as to why the suspect may have committed the act. When motive is not apparent and is the suspect's secret, they will sometimes play a little sadistic game with the interrogator. I seldom obtain confessions unless I told the suspect precisely why he committed the crime. They will resist confessing until you get it right. Unveiling the suspect's motivation has a profound psychological impact. The suspect loses his desire to compete with the interrogator on an intellectual basis. When you tell a suspect how he thinks, it creates a beneficial bonding between the interrogator and the suspect. The suspect gets the impression, "This guy understands me," and that thought, engenders respect for the interrogator. People don't generally confess to those they don't respect.

There is, however, one roadblock. Sometimes what the interrogator has to say can be accepted intellectually, but not emotionally. With some suspects, there is a strong suppression that deters a truthful verbalization of why they committed the crime. To counter this prohibitive factor, the interrogator can still get the job done by suggesting a less painful motive rather than the real one. This tactic makes it easier for the suspect to confess by avoiding the sinister aspect of the crime committed.

Despite the suspect's motive, it is disastrous for the interrogator to engage in condemnation. The wise interrogator creates the image of being an understanding person who does not personalize the interrogation by looking down on the suspect. Evincing empathy is a powerful tool of the astute interrogator. The emotional offender has a need to have someone listen. It is a truism that you tend to tell a good listener too much. That fact works to the benefit of the interrogator. It is amazing how many times people will confess because of the patience of the interrogator.

It is rare that in the life of an emotional offender he has the full attention of another human being who hangs on his every word. Psychologically, the interrogator's patience and listening ability can have an intoxicating effect on a suspect. Many suspects tell their attorneys that they confessed to the interrogator because he was a nice guy who showed understanding. With the emotional offender, the emotionally appealing arguments are the most effective. The rhetoric of a good interrogator can create the same emotional appeal as music.

The wrongdoer likes to hear that despite the act committed, they are not that evil. They like to hear that it was the provocation, rather than their character that prompted the act. One of my favorite arguments is to point out that there are certain life forces so powerful in nature that no rational thought process can control them. Anger is one of life's forces difficult to control. At times, we are all victims of anger. Suspects like to hear that everyone has problems with anger. That argument appeals to suspects because it brings into focus the old adage, "Misery loves company."

With the emotional fire-setter, it's effective to use the argument, "What you did is bad enough, why be a liar on top of it. Even prison inmates hate the liar. If I'm going to have any respect for you, it has to be based on your ability to tell the truth." The interrogator has to create a picture that lying about what the suspect did is almost as bad as the act itself. Many suspects will confess to gain some measure of respect from the interrogator.

I used the argument that there are certain life forces beyond the control of the rational thought process, to obtain the confession of a suspect who set fire to an Army Camp in New York State which caused the death of a serviceman. The suspect then fled New York, and set fires in many churches in different states before he was arrested in Miami. He was a compulsive fire-setter, and knew that he had a compulsion he couldn't control.

I used the argument of the difficulty of stemming uncontrolled rage, to obtain a confession from a woman who enticed men into hotel rooms. She would instruct the men to go into the bathroom to wash up. When they did, she would then set fire to the bathroom doors with lighter fluid. Her hatred of men created a scenario that the men least expected.

I used the argument, "What you did is bad enough, why be a liar on top of it," to obtain a confession from a fellow police officer who set fires to apartment buildings, hotels and office buildings in the downtown Miami area. That case was particularly embarrassing to our department. It was only solved because the fire marshall got suspicious of the officer because he was always around when the 40 odd fires occurred.

Fires to Defraud an Insurance Company

These cases are the most difficult for the interrogator, primarily because of the personality structure of the offender. Those who set fires to their houses or businesses, or have someone do it for them for monetary reasons, are generally shrewder and more articulate liars than the average emotional fire-setter. They generally have a history of defrauding individuals in various business transactions. Despite their failure in business, they have honed their basic instincts for social survival. Their materialistic nature manifests itself in calculating unlawful schemes.

I have obtained confessions in arson cases to defraud, but not many. In the cases where I was successful, there was just too much evidence for the suspect to lie. With the nonemotional offender, it's extremely difficult to get a confession when the evidence is solely circumstantial in nature. These cases are perplexing because sometimes it's not clear that an act of arson actually occurred.

In those instances where separate origins of fire have been established, or when a residue of an accelerant is present, an interrogator can feel comfortable that an act of arson was actually committed. As previously stated, you just can't interrogate with confidence if you have an element of doubt as to the subject's guilt or innocence. The clever, nonemotional fire-setter will always have a plausible explanation for the cause of the fire other than arson. Subjectivity plays a role in arson detection, and fire marshals are like polygraph examiners–the more experience they have, the smaller their margin of error.

With the nonemotional offender, and when the evidence is circumstantial in nature, there is a particular format that I would suggest the interrogator to follow. The main thrust of the interrogation is to get the suspect to lie about something that can be used later as a wedge to break him down. Success is based on the timing and the indepthness of the interview.

The interrogator has to give the impression to the suspect that the interrogator is just seeking information, and has an open mind. In the early stages of an arson investigation, the nonemotional offender will appear cooperative to give the impression that he has nothing to hide. They become belligerent and uncooperative if they are accused of being involved in setting the fire. The interrogator should not tip his hand until a detailed statement has been taken from the suspect. The best way for the interrogator to make up his mind as to the suspect's guilt or innocence, is to discover incriminating information in a detailed statement which covers the suspect's alibi, financial situation and any behavior out of the norm. Covering these particular areas will tell you if the suspect is on the defense or not.

When a liar keeps his story tight, and denies everything, leaving little to evaluate, his one Achilles' Heel is his alibi. This is particularly true when the suspect leaves town and has someone set the fire for him. The interrogator, in his questioning, has to evaluate whether or not the suspect's being out of town is coincidental or an effort to set up an alibi for the time of the fire. I've always been somewhat suspicious of people who are conveniently out of town when their home or business caught fire. To test the validity of the alibi, I suggest that the interrogator ask the following questions:

1. How long beforehand was the trip planned?

2. Who was with the suspect at the time of the trip?

3. Where did the suspect stay?

4. What was the purpose of the trip?

5. Did the suspect advise anyone that he was making a trip, and when did he do so?

6. Did the suspect make or receive any telephone calls while he was on the trip?

7. What purchases did the suspect make on the trip, and how did he pay for them?

8. Did the suspect ask anybody to check on his home or business while he was gone?

9. Did the suspect leave a pet with anybody while he was gone?

10. What personal papers did the suspect have on his possession at the time of the trip?

11. Did the suspect remove anything from his home or business that he did not take on the trip? [If the answer is no, this can later be contradicted by independent witnesses].

12. What personal items did you lose because of the fire in either your home or business?

13. How did you find out there had been a fire at your home or business?

14. Did anything unusual occur while you were on the trip other than the fire?

15. What is your theory as to how this fire occurred?

Innocent people, in discussing their alibi and the fire, generally manifest signs of anguish and bewilderment. In comparison, the guilty overdocument their alibi, and in most instances, display a dispassionate demeanor.

The second area that the interrogator should cover is the subject's financial background. Be leery of any suspect who becomes overly defensive or claims the questions are too personal in nature. It is suggested that the following questions should be asked:

1. Has his house or business been on the market for sale?
2. If so, for how long?
3. Has he reduced the price of his home or business in order to sell it?
4. What are the subject's mortgage payments, and what is the balance owed? How does this compare with his insurance coverage?
5. Was the suspect behind on his mortgage payments?
6. Has the suspect ever filed for bankruptcy?
7. Does the suspect have any legal judgments against him, or any pending lawsuits at the present time?
8. How much money does the suspect owe to creditors or suppliers?
9. Is the suspect in arrears in any tax payments?
10. How much money does the suspect have accessible to him at the present time?
11. What assets does the suspect possess beside cash?

The third area of inquiry should be questions concerning the suspect's insurance coverage and history. For example:

1. Has the suspect made any prior insurance claims? If so, for what, and what was the final disposition of any claim made?
2. Were any of the subject's prior insurance claims for fire?
3. What kind of insurance coverage did the subject have at the time of the fire, and with what companies?
4. Prior to the fire, did the suspect increase the amount of coverage on his home or business?
5. Prior to the fire, did the suspect buy any new insurance, such as Business Interruption Insurance?
6. How much is your claim, and how does that compare to what you owe on the building?
7. Have you hired a professional appraiser to evaluate your loss?

Remember that the whole purpose of covering these three areas is to invite the suspect to lie. If later investigation reveals that, in fact, the suspect did lie to one or more questions, then those lies become a wedge to be used in accusatory interrogation. Sometimes an arson suspect will do or say something that makes the probability of his guilt obvious. For example:

1. Buys or obtains an accelerant for no logical reason, other than for setting a fire.
2. Refuses to take a polygraph examination.
3. Simulates a forced entry to his home or business to throw suspicion on an outsider.
4. Claims that he had prior electrical problems or defective appliances, which necessitated bringing in a repairman. He will later place the blame on the repairman for causing the fire.
5. The owner will change an employee's work hours so that that employee will not become an inadvertent witness to the setting of the fire or might prematurely discover the fire before it does the intended damage.
6. Refuses to cooperate with the fire marshall, including the refusal to answer even the most innocuous questions.
7. Employer's overkill in directing suspicion to former employees who according to him, have motivation to set fire to his building.
8. Some suspects who fear being arrested for arson, will state that they are not going to make an insurance claim. This tactic, in

their mind, eliminates the potential charge of attempting to defraud an insurance company.

BURGLARY CASES

I never had much success interrogating professional safecrackers or jewel thieves, unless I had overwhelming evidence. No emotional appeal worked. Once they were given their Miranda Warning, the game was over. I did, however, have a lot of success with young burglars who were not yet institutionalized by previous imprisonment. Young burglars generally had the same profile. They were unsuccessful in academics and sports and did not have a good work ethic. To gain recognition, they turn to crime. The only thing they are enthusiastic about is the thrill they get from committing crimes. Crime satisfies their materialistic drive or it is a means to obtain funds to satisfy a drug habit.

In the interrogation of a young burglar, I would point out the crime is a youthful game, and most criminals when they reach around 40 years of age, have an attitude change when they realize that criminal activity obeys the law of diminishing returns. The lucky criminal eventually gets out of prison and many change their way of life, but some wind up spending all their lives in prison because they committed a more serious crime during the commission of a burglary such as murder, rape or assault. I like to point out to a young burglar he shouldn't wait until 45 years of age to change his attitude or risk permanent incarceration because on impulse he committed a serious crime during the commission of a burglary. I point out to a young burglar that if he is smart, and he has the fortitude, he can save himself of a wasted life by telling the truth about everything he has done, do his time and get out of prison while he is still young. In addition, the young burglar should be told if he tells the truth about all the burglaries he has committed and helps to recover some of what he has stolen, he will appear to be a good candidate for rehabilitation, particularly if he involves a fence. That adds to his degree of cooperation.

Prosecutors are generally cooperative in giving consideration to a young defendant who helps to land a bigger fish. In summation, I think it is important to point out to the young burglar that by telling the truth he takes control of his life and precludes the possibility of letting the system dictate his permanent fate.

I would like to reiterate that it is not necessary for an interrogator to be a psychologist. But, any argument created to induce a confession should be based on a common sense knowledge of human nature. In reference to young burglars, I've read some off-the-wall theories such as the burglar's access into a home through a window is symbolic of a return to the womb. I certainly wouldn't use that theory in an attempt to induce a confession. To me, I am more comfortable with the concept that all criminals have an attitude problem. They choose to dispel aggression and obtain recognition by socially unacceptable means. All human beings have the same basic drives. Good people satisfy these drives by socially acceptable means.

Chapter XI

CLOSURE–THE THREE TYPES

Closure is the first time you ask the subject for an acknowledgement of guilt. All of the interrogational arguments up to the point of closure are the preface to closure. Closure is a matter of timing. A good interrogator never closes until he feels his interrogational arguments have had an impact and the suspect is ready to confess. Premature closure commits the suspect to his lies. A delayed closure is like "talking past the sale."

Closure should be done when you begin to see or sense the buying signals: when you see the subject's head nodding in agreement, a welling-up of tears in the eyes or an overall appearance of resignation. Closure is the first time that you dramatically increase the force of the assertion of guilt. Closure must be done in a firm, positive manner giving the impression that you're not going to take no for an answer. It is a no-nonsense, positive demand for an acknowledgement of guilt. It is more of a statement than a question. A weak closure can negate the effectiveness of all of the interrogational arguments that preceded that moment.

It has been my experience that interrogators have more problems with closure than with any other phase of criminal interrogation. It's the first time the interrogator faces the possibility of failure. For this reason, some interrogators put off closure, afraid that the suspect is not going to acknowledge his guilt. It is terribly disappointing to an interrogator to use good interrogation arguments and then find out that they weren't good enough. Some interrogators are afraid to close for fear of turning an amicable relationship into one of animosity. Succinctly stated, they are reluctant to state, "You're lying through your teeth." An experienced interrogator knows he may have to close several times before getting an acknowledgement of guilt. Therefore, an interrogator should never show disappointment when a suspect fails to acknowledge his guilt after the first closure.

Even if the suspect doesn't admit his guilt after the first closure, the interrogator should never show any signs that he's going to give up or that he has any doubt as to the suspect's guilt. Confronted with denial, the interrogator should simply reiterate the previously used arguments and close again. There are three types of closure.

Going for the Jugular

In this type of closure, the interrogator asks for an immediate and complete acknowledgement of guilt. For example:

1. "You killed her, didn't you?"
2. "You stole the thousand dollars, didn't you?"
3. "You held up that store, didn't you?"

The benefit of this type of closure is the fact that you get a complete acknowledgement of guilt. The drawback is that sometimes it asks for too much too quickly. For that reason the second type of closure is generally more effective.

Admission of a Detail

In this type of closure, you ease the suspect into a full confession by getting him to admit a detail of the crime first. For example:

1. "You can take me to the gun that was used, can't you?"
2. "You were in the house with the little girl, weren't you?"
3. "You've got some of the money left, haven't you?"

Alternative Motives

In this type of closure, you provide the subject with the real reason for the crime and a second less incriminating one that suggests a mitigating factor for the act. For example:

1. "Did you plan to kill her before you picked her up or did you kill her because you suddenly realized by her threats that she could identify you?"

2. "Did you shoot the clerk to eliminate a witness or did you shoot him out of fear because when he made a motion to reach under the counter you thought perhaps he was reaching for a gun?"
3. "Had you been thinking about stealing that money or was it just an impulsive thing because someone was stupid enough to leave it out?"

This type of closure invites the suspect to confess in the best light. The drawback to this type is that it may lock a suspect into an untruthful story, which later forces the interrogator to talk the suspect out of the nice reason, rather than the real reason for his act. If the interrogator is successful in getting an acknowledgement of guilt to any of the three different types of closure his job is definitely not over.

HANDLING THE CONFESSION

If you are successful in closure and the suspect admits his guilt, the ballgame is not finished. How you handle the confession is just as crucial as how you conduct closure. If you don't do it correctly you can talk the suspect right out of confessing even if he has begun.

There are three types of confessors. The first is the suspect who wants to get it all off his chest and doesn't want to be interrupted while he's talking. You can turn him off by asking a bunch of premature questions because of your nervousness. A full, valid confession comes only one time, when the mood strikes the suspect. The chemistry has to be just right. When the suspect starts to confess the interrogator should give him his undivided attention. It's all right to nod in agreement or repeat a word or sentence the confessor uses, but don't impede the flow of the confession by asking questions. When he has completed his confession you should say to him, " I don't condone what you did but I admire your fortitude in telling the truth. I think I understand most of what you said, but there are a few points I want to clarify." At that point, the interrogator can ask as many questions as necessary.

The second type of confessor is the suspect who wants to test the water and wants to confess only on his own terms. He will lie about motive, shift blame or acknowledge only one crime, even though he has committed several. If the interrogator gets the impression early on that the suspect is only giving him "a piece of the pie," he should stop the suspect before he cements himself into his partial confession. The interrogator should hold up his hand and state, "Just a moment. I'm not going to accept that. The truth is not 65 percent, it's 100 percent. If you're going to tell the truth you should tell it all the way. Otherwise, you've accomplished nothing. A surgeon doesn't take out half a cancer, he takes it all out. You're not going to feel any better by making a token confession."

It should be noted, that many people suspected of a series of cash thefts will admit to one theft and then say they didn't do the others. They're trying to minimize their guilt as if to say, "OK, I confessed to one, if I did the others why wouldn't I admit them too?" This tactic holds true with other types of crimes as well. If the suspect is adamant in his token confession then you have to back off because of the possibility that he may retract everything he said. A partial confession is better than none at all.

The third type of confessor is the ambivalent confessor. He confesses and then states, "No, I don't see how I could have done it." He does this because he wants to tell the truth, but he's fearful of the consequences of confessing. When you proceed with additional interrogation, he will confess again. This type of confessor needs constant reassurance that he is doing the right thing.

This behavior can be exasperating to an interrogator because it is obvious that the suspect is guilty and he's trying to leave the door open for a retraction of the confession. With this type of confessor, the interrogator has to challenge the subject's fortitude. Point out that he "knows what he did and he should be man enough to tell the truth." Say, "You're not going to feel any better until you accept what you did and tell the truth about it. You can't play games with the truth."

Chapter XII

THE FORMAL CONFESSION
AS COURT EVIDENCE

The interrogator should not make the mistake of assuming that when he convinces a suspect to confess the ballgame is over. Many suspects will confess, and then refuse to give a written or recorded confession. Many suspects will make a truthful confession, but when they start thinking about the consequences of their acts, they look for a bail-out position. They don't want to lock themselves into a formal confession that can be used against them in a court of law. Criminals have a propensity for playing both ends into the middle.

To avoid this problem, the formal confession should be taken without delay while a suspect is in a cooperative mood. To make the transition to a formal confession, I suggest that the interrogator should make the following statement to a suspect:

> I am assuming that what you just told me is the truth. For your protection, I'm going to take a formal confession which will record exactly what you told me. By giving a formal confession, you will prevent anyone at a later date of exaggerating what you said, or accusing you of doing more than what you admitted. Your formal confession will be a record of your side of the story. If what you told me is the truth, it will be the truth no matter how it is recorded.

How the interrogator takes the formal confession depends on the resources available at the time the confession is taken. Sometimes I have the suspect write out his confession in his own hand. This type of formal confession has the appearance of voluntariness, but it is dependent on the suspect's writing skills. The major drawback of this type of confession is getting complete details of the suspect's act. It is a tedious process. Often, the suspect will say, "What do you want me to put down here?" I suggest that the interrogator replies, "You told me before you got the idea of stealing the money because the cash drawer was left open and no one was looking. If that's the truth, then write that down."

Many federal officers write down what the suspect confessed to, and then they have the suspect initial each page of the officer's writings indicating that the suspect agrees with what the officer wrote. Unfortunately, local police don't have the accompanying prestige of a federal officer. This technique, if used by a local police officer, invites questions as to its validity. The suspect can, at a later date, simply say, "He wrote it all down, and I didn't read it. I just initialed the pages because he told me to."

When a stenographer was not available, I generally obtained a formal confession by audio or video recordings. This is the best method for providing the judge and jury the atmosphere of the confession setting and the sincerity of the confessor. There is, however, one major drawback to this technique. In court, the interrogator is invariably asked during cross-examination, "Why didn't you record the entire interview of the defendant? What are you hiding from the jury?" I never felt entirely comfortable answering that question. I never said it, but I often wanted to say, "I didn't want to give you a sword you could stick in me."

There are two States that require that the entire interrogation of a criminal suspect be recorded. In my opinion, there is an inherent danger in that process. It is impossible, in my opinion, to conduct any interrogation without someone construing the interrogator's remarks as either a direct or indirect promise or threat. Such innocuous remarks as "Get this off your chest and you'll feel better" and "You'll never have peace of mind until you've told the truth," are viewed by some as a promise and a threat.

In commercial polygraph testing, the federal law requires that the person being tested be advised of the presence of recording equipment, and if it is to be used. Knowing that the entire session is going to be recorded has a definite effect on both the suspect and the interrogator. The tape recording exposes both to public disclosure, and that fear causes both the interrogator and the suspect to play-act. Both become stilted in their demeanor, and that is the antithesis of what you need for successful interrogation.

Suspects confess to someone they respect, and because of the camaraderie created between the suspect and the interrogator. Video recordings expose the suspect to the world, and they are not generally desirous of enduring that much shame. An interrogation session is a unique interpersonal relationship between the suspect and the interrogator. Any variable can destroy the chemistry necessary for the interrogator to be successful.

I prefer taking a formal confession by utilizing a stenographer. It's the confession that is least vulnerable to attack. The stenographer can place the suspect under oath, and she can later testify to the voluntariness of the confession. This format provides a more detailed confession because it is not restricted by the tiring process of handwriting. The typed confession has a more professional appearance.

The only drawback to this procedure is the length of time it takes for the stenographer to type the confession. On rare occasions, while the confession is being typed, the suspect starts thinking about the consequences of his act, and will sometimes refuse to sign the typed confession. The best way to prevent this occurrence is to keep up the continuity of the suspect's cooperation, by visiting the crime scene and recovering weapons or the fruits of the crime. Anything that is recovered, should be tagged and signed by the suspect. The interrogator should have the suspect write on the tag, "This is the weapon I used" or "The items I stole." This diversion of visiting the scene of the crime and collecting evidence, gives the stenographer time to type the confession. When the interrogator brings the suspect back to the station and the formal confession is ready to be signed, little resistance is generally encountered.

What the Formal Confession Should Contain

In cases where I obtained the confession, and the confession was introduced as evidence in a court of law, a certain procedure was followed. I read the questions asked of the suspect and, the prosecutor, playing the role of the suspect, answered the questions. This procedure was dramatic in nature, and in most instances, made an indelible impression in the minds of the jurors. When I took a formal confession, I always had in mind, "How is this going to sound in court?" Ideally, I wanted the confession to sound voluntary, be coherent in nature, and with sufficient details covering every aspect of the crime. I didn't want to be embarrassed by a failure to ask a pertinent question. In an important case such as murder, the interrogator can sometimes get nervous and forgetful. Thoroughness is dependent on good work habits. If an interrogator follows a definite format, he will avoid being embarrassed in a court of law.

Every formal confession taken by utilizing a stenographer should start with an introduction, or heading to the formal confession. For example, "This statement is being taken from Mr. John Doe in reference to the fatal stabbing of Mr. Joe Wilson that occurred at approximately 11:30 pm on September 15, 2001. The questions asked in this statement will be made by Detective Warren D. Holmes. Present at the time of the statement, and recording the questions and answers, is Stenographer Jane Brown. This statement is being recorded at 4:30 pm on September 16, 2001. The Case Number is 962531."

Following this introduction, the stenographer should place the suspect under oath. Following that, the Miranda Warning should be reiterated to the suspect, and that Warning should be done in a calm and business-like manner. The opening questions by the interrogator should be as follows:

1. "Mr. Doe, you and I had an earlier conversation regarding the death of Joe Wilson. Did you tell me the truth when you said that you killed Wilson and why you did it?" *Answer:* "Yes"
2. "Are you now willing to give a formal statement regarding your involvement in the death of Joe Wilson?" *Answer:* "Yes."
3. "Prior to taking this statement, has anyone made any promises to you, or threaten you in any way to make this formal confession?" *Answer:* "No."

In taking the formal confession, specific information should be obtained. The first sequence of questions should relate to the general personal background of the suspect. This sequence of questions establishes the fact that the information could only have come from the suspect. The answers received eliminate any future contention that the suspect never cooperated or volunteered any of the information contained in the confession. The following personal background questions are suggested:

1. "Please state your full name."
2. "What is your date of birth?"
3. "Where were you born?"
4. "What is your current address?"
5. "Are you married, single, divorced or separated?"

6. "What is the name of your wife or girlfriend?"
7. "Do you have any children?"
8. "What are their names and ages?"
9. "Were you ever in the military service?"
10. "Where were you last employed?"
11. "What was the name of your supervisor?"

Do not ask any questions regarding a prior arrest record, which would be prejudicial to the defendant and might disallow the formal confession. Do not ask any questions pertaining to other crimes previously committed, unless the crime was directly connected to the crime in question, and the purpose of taking the formal confession. If the suspect has committed multiple rapes or murders, the interrogator should take separate formal confessions for each crime committed. Do not ask any questions pertaining to illegal drug use, unless it has a direct bearing on the crime in question. Do not ask any questions pertaining to general mental health or prior psychological therapy. If the interrogator receives specific information regarding mental problems or prior psychological therapy, the interrogator should make separate notes of the information received, so that he can testify in court that he was aware of the subject's general background, but at the time he took the confession from him, he appeared to be coherent in nature.

Questions to Determine What Triggered the Crime

Questions in this category have to be done in a chronological order, so that the confession unfolds in a logical sequence of steps easily understood by a judge or jury. The questions should cover the following areas:

1. What was the suspect's relationship to the victim of the crime?
2. How long did the suspect know the victim?
3. In cases of armed robbery or burglary, why did the suspect pick that particular place to commit the crime?
4. Was the crime committed on impulse or thought-out beforehand?
5. How long did the suspect think about committing that particular crime?
6. Did the suspect tell anybody he was going to commit the crime?
7. Did the suspect have any particular plan to commit the crime?

8. Where did the subject get the weapon to commit the crime, or any tools, mask or ligatures?
9. Did he commit any crime to commit the crime in question, such as stealing a weapon or vehicle?
10. Did alcohol or illegal drugs play any role in the commission of the crime?

Questions Pertaining to the Location of the Crime

1. What relationship did the suspect have to the area or the building where the crime occurred?
2. If he did have a relationship, over what period of time?
3. What were the weather conditions at the time of the crime?
4. What were the lighting conditions at the time of the crime?
5. Who was present at the time of the crime?
6. Could anyone not involved in the crime have witnessed the crime?
7. Was the view obstructed so that no independent witness could have viewed the crime?
8. How did the suspect get to the area or the building where the crime occurred? For example car, bicycle, walking, bus, etc.
9. How did the suspect gain access to the building where the crime occurred?
10. Did the suspect have keys to the building?
11. Did the suspect observe any incident involving innocent people that occurred around the time of the crime? For example; a) a man walking a dog, b) a boy riding by on a bicycle [Incidental details lend credibility to a story, plus they provide potential witnesses].
12. Did the suspect do any damage to the building where the crime occurred?
13. Did the suspect remove anything from the building or the victim that did not belong to him?
14. Did the suspect leave any personal items that belong to him at the scene of the crime? [Suspects frequently leave personal items at the scene of a crime, for example, hats, coats, wallets, etc. The items a suspect sometimes leaves at a crime scene suggest a compulsion to be caught.]

Questions Pertaining to the Details of the Crime

In taking a formal confession, the interrogator should project himself to the scene of the crime, and should ask questions that make the crime unfold before his mind's eye. An interrogator, in taking the formal confession, should avoid filling in the voids of the suspect's story by suggestions. If the interrogator has difficulty with a void or reconciling an inconsistency, he should simply say to the suspect, "I don't understand. Why did you do that?" Forcing the suspect to be more explicit generally reconciles any discrepancy.

The interrogator's questions should keep the suspect on track, but the interrogator should not interrupt the suspect if he is submitting pertinent details and information. In obtaining the details of the crime, I suggest the following questions be asked:

1. What was the primary reason why the suspect committed the crime?
2. What was his mood at the time of the crime?
3. Did uncontrolled rage play any role in the crime?
4. Did alcohol or illegal drugs have any influence in the commission of the crime?
5. Did this victim say or do anything that initiated the suspect's act?
6. What remarks did the victim make during the commission of the crime?
7. What did the suspect say to the victim of the crime? [It should be noted that, when the interrogator covers conversations held and feelings, he automatically increases the voluntary appearance of the confession.]
8. Did the suspect do anything to hide his identity, such as wearing gloves, mask, etc?
9. What weapons were used in the crime, and where did they come from?
10. How many times did the suspect shoot the victim?
11. How many times did the suspect stab the victim?
12. Why did you shoot or stab the victim so many times?
13. Did you kill the victim to eliminate a potential witness?
14. Did you suffer any injuries during the commission of the crime?
15. What were all the things that the suspect did to ensure the victim's death?
16. How long was the suspect at the scene of the crime?
17. Did the victim offer any resistance?

Questions Pertaining to Post-Act Behavior

After the commission of the crime, perpetrators do strange things, from attempting suicide to buying flowers for their wives. The latter act emanates from a compensatory mechanism. The interrogator should ask questions to cover behavior that suggest it stems from guilt. In my opinion, the suspect should be asked questions covering the following acts:

1. Did the suspect do anything to hide the victim's body?
2. Did the suspect hide or give away any weapons used in the crime?
3. Did the suspect hide, sell or give away anything stolen from the victim?
4. Did the suspect think about committing suicide?
5. Did the suspect do anything in a reckless manner after the crime to put his own life in jeopardy? [Many suspects are so angry about their loss of self-control that caused the crime, they masochistically put themselves in a life-threatening posture.]
6. Did the suspect get drunk or buy illegal drugs?
7. Did the suspect do anything to compensate for his crime? For example, give money away or do something nice, which is out of character from his normal behavior.
8. Did the suspect admit his crime to any relative or acquaintance?
9. Did the crime cause the suspect to do anything different from his normal routine in life?

The Concluding Questions that Should Be Asked in the Taking of the Formal Confession

1. Is there anything you didn't tell me because I didn't answer the question?
2. Is there anything that you would like to add to this confession?
3. Have you been mistreated in any way?
4. Did you give this confession voluntarily and of you own free will?

Miscellaneous Factors to Be Recorded by the Stenographer

The interrogator should state:

1. "Let the record reflect that John Doe has drawn a picture of the crime scene."
2. "Let the record reflect that John Doe has identified the weapon used in the crime."
3. "Let the record reflect that John Doe has identified the items stolen from the crime scene."
4. "Let the record reflect that John Doe is crying."
5. "Let the record reflect that John Doe has left the room to go to the bathroom."
6. The stenographer should record the time the formal confession was concluded.

The Interrogator's Time Sheet

In preparation for trial testimony, the interrogator should make out what I call "The interrogator's Time Sheet." Notes should be made depicting the following information:

1. The time the initial interrogation began of the suspect.
2. Where the interrogation occurred.
3. Who was present?
4. The time the Miranda Warning was given.
5. How many times the suspect went to the bathroom.
6. What time did the suspect eat or drink anything.
7. The time the suspect made his first incriminating admission.
8. The time the suspect was brought to the crime scene to reenact the crime, and the time that weapons or the proofs of the crime were recovered.
9. The time the taking of the formal confession began and when it ended.
10. The time and date the suspect signed the formal confession.
11. What basic arguments were used to convince the suspect to tell the truth?

In my career, the prosecutors were always delighted when the defense attorney would ask me during a trial what I said to a suspect. They knew that by the defense attorney opening the door, I was going to make the closing argument for the state. In response to the defense attorney's question, I would get into evidence many incriminating facts precluded in my direct testimony.

The Final Tactic

Leave the suspect with a good taste in his mouth. Don't negate the rapport built with the suspect by making a demeaning remark after he signs the formal confession. That could lead to recantation and false accusations made by the suspect out of revenge. The interrogator should not give the appearance that he's won any victory. By maintaining good rapport with the suspect, the interrogator is sometimes awarded, at a later date, with additional admissions by the suspect to other crimes committed.

You Don't Always Need a Confession

Early in my career, I administered a polygraph examination to an electrician who got his wife drunk, attached some electric wires to her, and then electrocuted her. He insisted that his wife attached the wires to herself and committed suicide. I spent hours trying to get the suspect to admit he killed his wife. Unable to obtain a confession, I decided to take a formal statement from him and ask a multitude of questions that would make his guilt obvious based on his nonsensical replies to my questions.

Without a confession, the prosecutors were reluctant to prosecute the suspect. I insisted that the formal statement I took, and the absurdity of the suspect's answers, were sufficient. I further pointed out, that the electrician would never confess, and we should at least make him endure the anxiety of a trial.

Eventually, the prosecutors agreed to charge the suspect. At the trial, the formal statement was introduced with me reading the questions, and the prosecutor playing the role of the defendant, answering the questions. As I predicted, the formal statement had a tremendous impact on the jury. After debating for a short period of time, they reached a verdict of guilty. After the trial, the prosecutors questioned many of the jurors about their verdict, and what they believed. Each one told the prosecutor that among the jurors, there was one overwhelming single belief: "The suspect's answers to my questions made his guilt obvious."

I learned from that case, that you don't always need a confession if you can convey guilt by thorough questioning. Failure to get a confession should not be an excuse for an interrogator not to take a formal statement.

Chapter XIII

THE INTERROGATION OF
THE ACCOMPLICE

When you have more than one person suspected of being involved in a crime, the interrogator has to turn one participant against the others. That tactic ensures conviction.

From bitter experience, one word of caution should be noted: When the interrogator makes the decision as to who is going to be the defendant and who are going to be the witnesses, make sure the deals that are made are not made with the wrong person. In too many cases, the actual shooter winds up testifying against co-defendants who played a lesser role in the crime. The lying witness will frequently project his guilt on others.

Some potential witnesses, out of revenge, will lie about co-defendants, others will embellish the story to ingratiate themselves with the interrogator. Some will say anything to protect themselves. Be careful of the accomplice who fills in the voids by confabulation rather than actual knowledge. The interrogator has to be careful that the promises that are made will not invalidate the confession. If an accomplice tells the truth, it's only fair that consideration should be given to him for his cooperation.

It takes finesse to break down a lying accomplice, and to get them to agree to testify against others. The interrogator has one psychological factor in his favor, and that is the fact that most human beings are governed by the self-interest principle. That principle should be the framework for the interrogational arguments to be employed in getting one of the suspects to confess.

Each suspect has in common the fear that someone is going to talk to save themselves. The interrogator should take advantage of that fact. The suspect should be told that someone in the case is going to talk. He should be told that he is being talked to first because the interrogator believes that he played a lesser role in the crime and is capable of telling the truth. It should be pointed out to the suspect that if he chooses to lie, then someone else will put all the blame on him. The suspect should be told that the only obligation he has is to his family, and not to his co-defendants.

I like to point out to an accomplice, "Don't be a foolish martyr. It won't be appreciated, and you will regret it at a later date. You will find out that when you're walking around in a prison yard, the co-defendants will laugh and say that you were foolish for not taking the deal that they would have taken if they had been approached first." The interrogator should point out to the suspect that many people, particularly inmates, are ingrates. The suspect should be told, that by lying he's not being noble, he's just hurting himself. The suspect should be told, that by lying it's going to appear that he played a major role on the crime, and perhaps picked the place to rob, and knew in advance that there would be a shooting. The suspect should be told, if he tells the truth there'll be no mistake as to what actual role he played in the crime.

If one of the suspects decides to confess, the interrogator has one additional problem. It's been my experience that too often, the confessor does not tell the whole truth, primarily by minimizing his own role in the crime. For that reason, I always use the following argument:

> I don't condone what you did, but I respect the fact that you're man enough to stop the lying. I'm concerned, however, that you haven't told me the whole truth. If the prosecutor decides to give you consideration for being cooperative and to use you as a witness, he's not going to do either one if there is some question as to whether or not you told the whole truth. You will only be a good witness if you sound and look like you're telling the truth, and that's not possible if you know in your heart you haven't told the whole truth. The truth is not 85%, it's 100%. While sitting in court as a witness, there will only be two people in that courtroom who will know the whole truth, you and the guy you're testifying against.

> If you lie about anything, the defendant will whisper that fact to his defense attorney. When that attorney gets up to cross-examine you, he will know and you will know that he knows what you lied about.

Under cross-examination, if you lie, you will hurt the State's case, we don't want that. The State wants to bring out, in your direct testimony, everything you did in this case, so that the defense attorney has nothing to make you appear like a liar. So, if you picked the place to rob, or you're the one who took the money out of the cash register, you should state that fact and let's get that out of the way before this case goes to trial.

Now, there's one other thing. I want to put your mind at rest. The person you testified against, will only hate you if you lie, particularly if you put something on him you did. Oh! He won't love you for testifying against him, but if you tell the whole truth, his anger will subside. In time, he'll accept the fact that you did what you had to do, and if he was in your position, he would have done the same thing. However, if you lie, his anger will never die. A year from now, when you look back, you'll know that you made the right decision by telling the truth, and you'll have the satisfaction of knowing you told the whole truth.

I hope you understand what I just said, because I'm concerned you haven't told me everything, and you won't feel right until you do. Now, what is it that you didn't tell me?

Over the years, I've used that argument numerous times, and in most instances, got additional admissions as a result of using it. In view of the percentage of times that suspects don't initially tell the whole truth, I think it's imperative that the interrogator use some form of my argument.

THE INTERROGATION OF THE POTENTIAL WITNESS

This section pertains to the persons who might have knowledge of a crime, but did not participate in the actual commission of the crime. The potential witness may have seen it occur, heard about it, or perhaps, one of the actual perpetuators confessed to him their involvement in the crime.

There are several reasons why potential witnesses are reluctant to tell what they know.

1. They don't want to inform on a friend or relative.
2. They don't want to be put into a position of having to testify against a friend or relative.

3. They want to create a macho image, and later brag that they lied to the police.
4. They just don't want to get involved.
5. They identify with the suspect by race, gang membership and social standing.
6. They just don't like the police or any form of authority.

To co-op the potential witness, the approach has to be low key and disarming. The interrogator should use the subtle tactic of invoking guilt feelings in the witness. Point out to the potential witness that, if something happened to them, they would be furious that justice did not prevail because someone refused to reveal what they knew. Point out to the potential witness that he has a moral obligation to tell the truth. In addition to that, tell the witness that it is not a question of squealing on anyone, it's just a matter of doing what's right.

If the witness is intractable, then the interrogator has to become more assertive. Tell the witness he has an obligation to his family not to get into trouble protecting a criminal suspect. Tell the potential witness that if he doesn't tell you the truth, then you'll have no alternative but to place him under oath before an assistant state attorney or grand jury. Tell the witness this could lead to the potentiality of a perjury charge if at a later date, the actual perpetrator confesses and tells the police that the witness knew what happened. Tell the witness, that by lying he's acting more like an accomplice than just a witness. The interrogator should tell the potential witness that by lying, he also faces the possibility of being charged as an accessory before or after the fact.

The interrogator, to become more assertive, should accuse a recalcitrant witness of being involved in the commission of the crime. The interrogator should point out to the witness this is the only logical explanation for why he's lying about what he knows. Many potential witnesses, afraid of being arrested or being unjustly accused, tell what they know out of self-defense. If that tactic fails, then the interrogator has to make a deal with the potential witness. I suggest the following argument:

> It's obvious to me you just don't want to testify as to what you know. OK. I got an idea that will help both of us. I'm gonna let you tell me confidentially what you know, and you won't have to testify. I'm not going to tell anybody what you told me. By telling me confidentially what you know, you will not only be doing what is right, but you will eliminate being charged with withholding information at a later date.

This last-ditch effort to get the witness to talk has worked for me on numerous occasions. Its value is the fact that you received nothing initially from the witness prior to making the deal. If the witness talks with the promise of confidentiality, the interrogator opens the road to other potential witnesses and information as to how the crime was committed. The confidential information can also be used to retrieve weapons that were used in the crime, and the fruits of the crime.

Ironically, when a witness tells you something confidentially, it conditions him to become even more cooperative. Without violating the deal that you made with the potential witness, sometimes, of their own volition, they agree to testify.

Chapter XIV

COMMERCIAL THEFT CASES

EMPLOYEE THEFTS

Thirty-five percent of all businesses that go out of business do so because of employee theft. These cases are more challenging to an interrogator than most crimes because of the lack of physical evidence such as fingerprints, ballistics, DNA, etc. Generally, there is no direct evidence in the form of witness testimony. The most you can hope for is circumstantial evidence pointing to a particular suspect. In most instances, the interrogator is confronted with a substantial cash or merchandise loss with multiple suspects which is worse than having no suspects. The project becomes a fishing expedition. It is the job of the interrogator to pick out the thief and confirm that analysis by obtaining a confession.

I have worked on almost every type of criminal case, but I like these cases the best. They test your wits, people reading ability, and insight. The interrogator has to know the potential problems that will make his task difficult. He has to know the profile of the employee thief, questions to ask each employee, and the interrogational argument to be used once the employee responsible for the thefts has been identified.

Potential Problems

The first problem is the person giving you the case facts. Preferably, you should get your information from the owner of the business. Even then, some owners will tell you that a particular employee is not a suspect because he is not smart enough. Some owners don't want to believe they got outsmarted by a truck driver. Be leery of information received from a supervisor no matter how high their position in the company. They may have a vested interest in the case not being solved. The loss could be an embarrassment to them, either because of personal involvement or the theft reflects on their job proficiency.

Some supervisors will attempt to direct you away from favorite employees or someone they were intimate with. Some will fail to tell you that they received information regarding an employee's suspicious behavior because they are embarrassed that they failed to act on the information received. Some supervisors will not reveal the fact that they hired a particular employee despite having derogatory information regarding the employee. Some supervisors view themselves as protectors of their employees, which negates doing what is best for the business. They will tell you that an outsider probably committed the thefts when it was obvious it was an inside job. They will tell you that certain procedures were followed when they know for a fact they weren't.

They will naively or deliberately withhold from you prior shortages of cash or merchandise that could reveal a pattern or pinpoint an employee who is the common denominator in all of the losses. Some supervisors will suggest that employees may do poorly on a polygraph test for some reason other than lying. Remember that the theft is always a reflection on someone and therefore that someone has motive to give misinformation.

Clues to Look for

The interrogator should never assume he is dealing with a singular theft. If in fact he is, the task is more difficult. Even a miniscule theft preceding the big one can establish a common denominator and that generally outweighs all other circumstantial evidence. It is true that someone could be a victim of circumstance by their position but most of the time a person linked to a series of thefts by opportunity, time and place raises the statistical probability of guilt. For this reason, it is imperative for the interrogator to determine who was present at the time of the first theft. By the same token, a suspect can be eliminated if he or she has an irrefutable alibi for the time period of the thefts. Some people who have an appealing suspect in mind but that suspect has an alibi for one of the thefts, reconcile the problem by assuming someone else could have committed that theft. That rarely occurs. Most of the time, one person is responsible for all of the thefts. This is particularly true if the business has not sustained past acts of dishonesty. I can't overemphasize the importance of establishing the common denominator, the person who could have committed each theft in question. Determining the common denominator is your best interrogation wedge. Even a good liar can't lie around the fact that no one else but him or her could have committed the thefts in question.

If a business has had no prior thefts and suddenly there is a substantial loss of cash or merchandise, most of the time the culprit is the newest employee or some one hired around the same time. If there has been a series of thefts from employee pocketbooks, the thief to obscure her acts, will make up a story that someone stole from her purse. Be suspicious of the second or third alleged victims in a series of thefts from purses. Many times an owner or supervisor will state that their bookkeeper is sloppy but they don't think she is stealing. It's been my experience that many bookkeepers who steal are sloppy by design. Their deliberate sloppiness is done so to avoid detection.

The interrogator should look for who has the ultimate control. If that person did not commit the theft, he should be able to tell you who are the best suspects. For example, if a pharmacy is suffering losses of expensive drugs and the head pharmacist has no theory as to who stole the items, I'm going to be looking at him with a fish eye. The person in control knows the operation like the palm of his hand. If he knows he didn't do it by simple logic he can pinpoint the best suspect. A dishonest person who has control, can commit the thefts without fear of detection by devious manipulation.

The cause for many thefts are mistakes made by employees. They inadvertently leave money exposed, fail to lock the safe, or leave merchandise in the wrong place making it accessible to theft. These mistakes give the opportunist the chance to steal with the thought, "I can steal this and not be suspected." The interrogator has to be aware that many employees will lie about a violation in procedure in fear of being fired or appearing inefficient. Many times, I have obtained confessions that revealed that a fellow employee's mistake triggered the theft. This was the same employee that said he or she did everything right. You learn after being misled not to take for granted the testimony of employees who can't accept the fact that they did something wrong which facilitated the theft. An interrogator has to assume, despite assurances, that something out of the ordinary occurred that made the theft possible.

The interrogator should look for "the cushion factor." Most thefts, particularly in banks, are done on Friday. This allows the wrongdoer a weekend to mentally cope with the guilt and to create a defense. Many thefts are committed before a day off, vacation time, or a pending trip. Many persons who steal call in sick the next day or find a reason to resign shortly after the theft.

"The cushion factor" comes into play when several people had a potential role in handling the missing money. For example, the first person in the scenario can have the thought, "There will be others to go in the safe after me so I can steal some of this money with the defense that others went into the safe after me." The last person in the scenario can use the same cushion factor by thinking, "I can steal some of the money because three people went into the safe before me."

THE PROFILE OF THE EMPLOYEE THIEF

I don't believe that people by nature are honest, to the contrary, by nature they are basically acquisitive. This nature probably stems from the influence of the evolutionary process wherein it was necessary for ancient people to acquire and hoard in order to survive the winter months or periods when food was not readily available. Being honest is a learned process dependent on the development of a good superego. Conscience is the built-in police officer, inculcated by the influences of elders, schools, and religion.

It is amazing to me the number of times I have heard a young teller say, "You know Mr. Holmes, to me its not money, I'm just counting paper." Why the mental gymnastics if there is no need to suppress an ancient instinctive desire? People who are honest continually reinforce their honesty by self-pride. Their wealth is self-respect. The need for self-recognition is just as powerful to create honesty as it is to prompt someone to commit a crime for recognition. Both ways, it's always the factor of recognition.

In most instances, the case facts will dictate the personality structure of the perpetrator. The interrogator has to ask himself the question; did someone make a mistake which created too much temptation for someone who otherwise would not plan to steal? Did some poor soul, buffeted by personal problems, reach a point of despair where he or she through a theft might lessen their burdens? Some reach a point when they don't care anymore and adding the stigma of theft for them would not make matters worse. These people are situational thieves and not chronic thieves.

If you have a series of well-thought-out thefts, that is a different ball game and a different profile. That profile has become familiar to me, having worked on many employee theft cases. The person I have in mind is a chronic thief. They go from job to job and steal on each one. In fact, no window of opportunity to steal escapes them. They have a basic philosophy that everyone is dishonest. They further justify their thefts by finding a real or imagined grievance against their employer. Most of them have never seen the inside of a police station. They are smart and they confine their wrongdoing acts to the familiar territory of a job setting. This particular profile covers their behavior with a facade of normal family life. Their opiate is materialism. They like the nice things in life and they like to project the appearance of success by their possessions most of which has been obtained by stealing from employers. They are tough-minded and good liars. It has been my experience that there is a high correlation between constant lying and thievery. Under interrogation, they are generally glib, a necessary talent in order to be a good liar.

They are obsessed with recognition and Monday mornings regale fellow employees with fabricated stories about their weekend experiences. They love to ingratiate themselves with fellow employees. They are quick to loan money and to treat fellow employees to lunch. They play both ends to the middle by berating management when talking to fellow employees but are obsequious in the presence of management. In general conversation they project a know-it-all attitude and actually believe they are smarter than everybody else is. Their tough-mindedness enables them to show no signs of guilt generally observed in an inexperienced thief. They try to be the dominant personality in the building. Fortunately for the interrogator, they do have an Achilles heel. What they are does not escape the notice of fellow employees. To me, fellow employees are the best lie detector. Eighty-five percent of the time, some employee has given me the information which pinpointed the thief. The information received was always in response to several questions designed to reveal the profile previously described. It is suggested that you set up the questions I have in mind in the following way.

I am not asking you to accuse anyone because we are discussing the matter in general terms, but I have great faith in the judgment of employees and their evaluation of someone they work beside eight hours a day, five days a week. So, I need your help. If you are right, you can help me solve this case. If you are wrong, no harm is done because you are not accusing anyone, you are just answering my questions. Truthfully, who do you and other employees think is tough-minded enough to steal the missing money even if he didn't do it?

The follow-up questions should be:

1. Is there anyone here who the employees think has a habit of taking undue liberties with the truth?
2. Who do you think is not tough-minded enough to steal the missing money?
3. Is there anyone here who seems to be always telling outlandish stories as an attention-getting device?
4. Is there anyone here who has a general reputation of being a manipulator?
5. Is there anyone here that, regardless of the discussion, gives the impression that he or she is always right?
6. Is there anyone here who tries to dominate other employees?
7. Is there anyone here who brags about what they have, what they just bought, or what they intend to buy?
8. Is there anyone here who seems to be constantly negative about everything concerning their job?

WHAT TO LOOK FOR DURING THE INTERVIEW

When a person tells the truth, they generally look and sound like they are telling the truth. When you interview several employees and suddenly you encounter an employee employing obvious defense mechanisms, they stick out like a sore thumb. If a person is on the defense, what you see mostly is hostility and evasiveness. The third red flag is a dispassionate demeanor. You see hostility because people hate what they fear. You see evasiveness because the guilty use a thinking-away process to divorce themselves from the emotional counterpart of the act committed. A subject with a dispassionate demeanor is in an emotional neutral slot. They are devoid of the normal passion and curiosity of one trying to figure out, "Who did this?" A feigned, unconcerned attitude toward a significant event is not normal and should be looked upon with suspicion. If you interview 20 people and three manifest any of the described defense mechanisms, the thief is probably one of the three. The other two are hiding unrelated guilt feelings or personal problems that could be a source of embarrassment to them.

My favorite defense mechanisms are overexclusion and projection. When I see either one of these particular defense mechanisms in an employee, in conjunction with the others already described, I get the idea I got my culprit. In my mind people who make declarations of exclusion to a point of absurdity have little credibility. What they try to do is to convince the interrogator that there is no way they could have committed the crime. They make this argument despite the fact that they had access to the missing money and could have stolen the money without detection. To test to what degree they will exclude themselves I will often ask, "Well, you had the keys to the office and the combination to the safe, so if you wanted to steal the money, you could have." The truthful person will respond, "Yes, I could have, but I didn't." The guilty, as a rule, seldom acknowledge they could have stolen the money. Those who use the defense mechanism of projection will attempt to misdirect your inquiry. They will project their guilt on an innocent person to divert suspicion away from themselves. They use rumors, misinformation and circumstances to direct suspicion to others. Sometimes they project their guilt on management. They will state that they don't think the money was stolen, it's just a paper error. They will further contend that all the employees are honest and therefore there could be no theft. This contention automatically excludes them from suspicion. Anyone who is too dogmatic in their interview, without any degree of objectivity indicates that the suspect is using overkill to misdirect the interrogator.

GENERAL QUESTIONS TO BE ASKED OF EACH EMPLOYEE

1. How long have you worked here?
2. What is your job?

3. When did you first find out about the missing money?
4. What were you doing during the time period the money disappeared?
5. Was that your normal routine? [Be wary of people who do something different. They may have changed their routine to set up an alibi.]
6. Did you work your normal hours on that day? [Many people leave the job early after committing a theft]
7. What time did you eat lunch and did you take any other breaks?
8. Did you go to your car for any reason before you left work? (Some employees will hide in their car what they stole.]
9. Do you have keys to the building?
10. Do you have the combination to the safe?
11. Are you ever alone in this building before or after normal hours?
12. Do you ever enter the building on weekends?
13. Do you ever have any visitor on the job? [Many who steal pass the stolen money or merchandise to a friend or relative]
14. When you left work, the day the money disappeared, did you go straight home or some place else? [Anything different from going straight home is significant. Post-act behavior can be an indication that the suspect was dealing with unusual stress].
15. What is the most expensive item you have purchased in the last six months?
16. What was the biggest bill you have paid in the last six months? [With these two questions, the thrust of the questioning is to get the employee to acknowledge the source of money that he used for purchases or paying bills which he cannot explain. The unexplained money becomes a wedge in the interrogation process.]
17. What are your monthly financial obligations? [Find out if they are behind in rent or mortgage payments, car payments, credit card and etc. [A dire financial position could be a motive for committing the crime in question.]
18. "I want you to think carefully before you answer this question." [Ask the question like you already know the answer]. "Have you ever been fired for stealing, accused of stealing or questioned about stealing on a prior job?" [If the answer is in the affirmative, that might indicate that they have a propensity to commit the theft in question. If the response is no to each question and

you later find out they lied, that creates a strong argument that if they lied about their background, they could be lying in their denial of stealing the money in question.]

19. Did anything unusual occur on the day the money disappeared, which could have diverted people's attention, giving someone the opportunity to steal the missing money?
20. Was there any violation of security that could have caused the theft?
21. Do you know of any fellow employee who is having financial problems?
22. Has any employee bought anything or paid any bill when you wondered where they got the money?
23. Since this happened, has anyone been acting differently or acting like the cat that ate the canary?
24. Is there anyone who seems overly concerned about the theft and constantly talks about it?
25. Has anyone told you that they suspect a particular individual of committing the theft.
26. Did anyone leave early on the day of the theft? [Thieves get nervous and want to get off the jobsite].
27. Did anyone disappear for a period of time and you wondered where they were?
28. Did any one appear too unusually upset after the theft?
29. Did anyone not show up for work after the disappearance of the money?
30. Have you ever been convicted of a crime?
31. Recreationally, have you used any illegal drugs? [Don't ask questions 30 and 31 until you have established a rapport with the employee].
32. Confidentially, is there anyone that you suspect?
33. What is your theory about the missing money? [This is the most important question I ask. It reveals that the employee is comfortable discussing the crime or engages in disassociation].
34. Is there anything you didn't tell me because I didn't ask you the question? [This is always the last question you ask. Many people will withhold pertinent information with the excuse, "Well, he didn't ask me the question"].

THE TRANSITION FROM NONACCUSATORY TO ACCUSATORY INTERROGATION IN COMMERCIAL THEFT CASES

If an interrogator receives obvious discrepancies between what an employee said and the testimony of others, that can lead to a solution of the case if it is a factual difference rather than a difference in subjective analysis. The differences in testimony, particularly if it is several against one, can be used as a wedge to get a confession. When you reach a conclusion as to who you think committed the theft, then you have to make a transition from nonaccusatory interrogation to accusatory. This is easy if a polygraph test has been administered because all you have to do is tell the suspect he was untruthful on the test. If no polygraph testing was done, then the transition takes finesse.

One word of caution, if you don't know for a fact that the person you are talking to stole the missing money, but circumstantially it appears that way, you still have to attempt the transition to accusatory interrogation. However, at the same time you have to leave yourself with a bailout position if you change your mind about the suspect. A good interrogator can change directions with both feet off the ground. Thus. in my opinion, the transition should be done in the following manner.

> As you know I am interviewing all of the employees who could have stolen the missing money. At this point, I cannot clear you of this theft. There are some things about you that are disturbing to me. You definitely had the opportunity to steal the missing money. You also appear troubled to me. For the moment, let us assume that you are having some personal problems that are overwhelming. Under ordinary circumstances, I would not expect you to do anything wrong, but under pressure, good people succumb to temptation assuming that the theft of money might help their personal problems. This could be the case with you. If you did in fact steal the missing money, then it's just a question as to whether or not you have the fortitude to tell the truth.

At this point, the interrogator has to evaluate the reaction of the suspect to what has just been stated. Innocent people, in response to the transition argument, show a look of disbelief and exasperation. They are quick to protest. You will also note that as you are talking, there is an uneasiness in their demeanor because they know what you are saying has no application to them. If you see this, then you may have to back off. The guilty on the other hand, become more subdued and listen with an intensity, obviously weighing their response. You look for the buying signals, and they can be many. There may be a slumping in posture, a welling up of tears in the eyes, and the nodding of the head in assent. If you see these signs, then the interrogator has to become more assertive in his arguments.

SUGGESTED ACCUSATORY ARGUMENTS

"The Common Denominator" Argument

> I am convinced you stole the missing money. In fact, no one else could have stolen the money. You are the common denominator in this case. Now let me tell you the position you are in. What happens to you in this case is dependent upon your degree of cooperation. I don't think you would hold up a liquor store or break into a house, but by lying you place yourself in the same league with common criminals. I don't think you want to give that image. You are not going to like yourself unless you have corrected the wrong you have committed. You can only do that by telling the truth. You will find out it's just too much work and not worth it to lie to yourself and others for the rest of your life. To gain back your self-respect, you have to show you are sorry for what you did and if possible, pay back what you stole. If you can't pay the money back, at least lessen your wrongdoing by telling the truth. I don't think that you are a bad person. Your personal problems caused you to do something you would not do under ordinary circumstances. What you thought might be a solution to your personal problems, in reality created a lifetime burden of guilt. Lying always perpetuates guilt feelings. I am talking to you because I don' t think you like what you did and I think you are capable of telling the truth. You are better off suffering the temporary embarrassment of telling me what you did than suffering guilt feelings for the rest of your life. I am sure there is a logical explanation for why you took the money. Now, you did steal the money, didn't you?

"Misery Loves Company" Argument

> Let me explain something to you I don't think you understand. Eighty-five percent of employees steal merchandise from employers,

from minor to expensive items. Sixty-five percent of employees steal money in various amounts, from pennies to large amounts of cash. I am telling you this because I don't want you to think that you are alone in this type of behavior. I don't condone what you did, but I understand it. We all know we shouldn't steal, but every once in a while the braking system slips. That's because of the frailty in human nature. All people have an acquisitive nature. That means a desire to collect things. We inherited that from the evolutionary process. We spend a lifetime fighting our own basic nature. Under sufficient provocation, anyone is capable of stealing. The only difference between you and those that don't steal, is that you slipped a little bit. Today you have the opportunity to get back on the right track by showing you are not a liar on top of what you did. Most people will forgive you for what you did, providing you don't insult their intelligence by lying.

"If You Lie, You Win No Victory" Argument

My report is going to indicate you stole the missing money, so if you walk out of here without telling me the truth, you have won no victory. I get paid whether you tell the truth or not. If I thought you were really a bad person, I wouldn't waste my time talking to you. I get the impression that you are capable of telling the truth if I can just convince you that by lying you are only making a bad situation worse. When you commit a crime there are only three things you can do. Be sorry for what you did, try to make amends by restitution and forget what you did. If you don't do that, you imprison yourself in the jailhouse of your own mind. One way or another, we all pay for our sins. Even the Bible points out that ill-gotten gain profits no man. You have to ask yourself how you feel now compared to how you felt before you stole the money. The most precious thing that human beings possess is their self-respect. You won't get yours back until you tell the truth. By committing the theft, you have violated the basic principles by which you have abided all of your life. Don't let this single wrongdoing dictate what you are for the rest of your life. If you have no intention of being a criminal, then you shouldn't act like one. People are evaluated not by a single incident in their life, but their total existence. It's how you finish the race that counts. What you did can be eradicated by getting back on the right track and to do that, you have to tell the truth. If you walk out of here without telling the truth you have committed the worst crime of all, a wasted life.

INTERNAL BANK THEFTS

During my career, I have worked on many cases involving internal bank thefts. You would assume that the commonality of banking procedures and the historical development of security means would preclude major theft problems. That has not been the case. Despite hiring the best people possible, banks still get hit periodically with sizeable thefts of money. Succinctly put, the thefts occur because of breakdowns in security measures or someone bent on stealing who is not deterred by any form of security.

Most of the interrogational arguments already stated in this chapter have application in the interrogation of any bank employee suspected of stealing from a bank. I believe however, that there are aspects unique to internal bank thefts that should be known to an interrogator. First, it has been my experience that there is a direct correlation between the person's position in a bank and how much they steal. The higher their position, the more they steal.

Those who steal from banks generally fall into two categories, those who steal from their own cash drawers and those who steal from other tellers, the main vault or bank deposit bags. In the first situation, the background is always the same. The teller is having financial and other personal problems and starts stealing small amounts of money from their own cash drawer. At the end of the work shift, they then balance showing no shortage or overage. They can't keep forcing balances because in most banks there are periodic audits of money entrusted to tellers. Realizing that they are going to be caught with a shortage of funds, they make up the story that they balanced short $2,000 and must have inadvertently handed it out during a large transaction. They will either tell that story or contend that they left the cash drawer unattended and someone may have stolen the money from their cash drawer. In most instances during the interrogation, this subject is vulnerable to the argument, "It was not your character that caused the theft, but your personal problems."

In contrast, if several tellers sustain shortages when they balance and they have no history of prior shortages, this indicates an opportunistic thief is working in the bank. This type of thief moves from teller cage to teller cage, under the pretense of just visiting or to buy or sell money. When the victim's attention is diverted, the thief makes a fast grab and secretes the money. The bravado of this type of thief has always fascinated me. You learn that whatever temerity it took to commit the thefts, is coupled with an ability to mask their guilt. They generally fit the profile of the chronic thief already portrayed in this chapter. Needless to say, they are more difficult to interrogate than the poor soul who steals because of overwhelming personal problems.

PINPOINTING THE THIEF

To pinpoint the person responsible for stealing from different tellers, you have to ascertain who is the common denominator. The fact that they exchanged money with a fellow teller can be documented. However, when they enter another teller's area to converse and then commit a theft, they frequently deny talking to the victim on the day of the shortage. To counteract this problem, I have frequently used the tactic of bluffing. It is done in the following manner.

> You said that you didn't go into Mary's work area on the day she had the shortage. She believes you did. I want you to think about that carefully because we intend to take fingerprints from her cash buggy. Now if you did in fact visit Mary on that day and you touched or leaned against her buggy, we will undoubtedly find your fingerprints which could have been left there during an innocent conversation.

If the suspect, after hearing this, decides to change her story, be wary of that individual. Particularly, if she is adamant in her denial of going near the victim's cage. Many banks use cash buggies that the tellers wheel out from the main vault at the beginning of the work shift and return it back to the main vault at the conclusion of their work shift. Tellers generally keep their loose bills in their working cash drawer and their strapped money in the buggy. The buggy is kept adjacent to them while they face the teller window. If the victim's attention is diverted while waiting on a customer, the thief has an opportunity to make a fast grab of money from the buggy.

SIGNS OF GUILT

There are several behavioral indicators generally associated with guilt. One is a teller who says that they are not responsible for the loss of money but feel morally obligated to make up the loss. It's possible, in a rare situation, this statement can be made by an innocent person. It's been my experience that better than 90 percent of the time, the person making this statement stole the missing money. This offer is a means of guilty people placating their guilt without going so far as to confirm it with a confession.

Another indicator of guilt are those tellers who display a dispassionate demeanor without evincing concern for their shortage. Honest tellers, in contrast, show great concern because they view the shortage as a reflection on their job proficiency or honesty. They will make such remarks as, "I couldn't sleep all night, I drove my husband nuts trying to figure this out.

In the pursuit of truth, I've always been jealous of innocent people. They have an advantage over everybody else. They know they didn't do it and nobody else can make that statement. Because they know they didn't commit the act, they demonstrate an insatiable curiosity in trying to figure out who or what caused the shortage.

A third indicator generally associated with guilt are tellers who display mood swings while being interviewed. They attempt to simulate innocence by an obsequious demeanor and then become suddenly defiant if they get the impression you disbelieve them.

Most tellers who steal do so on a Friday. They balance around 2:00 pm and then reopen for customers around 4:00 pm. Friday's late afternoon transactions are then carried over to Monday's work, and by not balancing before opening Monday morning, they extend the time period during which the shortage could have occurred. A theft committed on Friday automatically carries with it cushion time for the thief. Without a confession, you will never know if the money was stolen Friday or Monday.

WHY THEY STOLE

Over the years, I've been given many explanations for why tellers stole while employed at a bank. Examples are:

1. They stole from a particular customer because they knew the customer had a reputation in the bank for frequently making mistakes in deposits.

2. A traumatic event occurred in their life, such as separation from their husband or illness in their family. They just got to a point where they didn't care anymore.
3. They had to pay for car repairs or if they didn't, they couldn't get to work.
4. They were behind on rent or mortgage payments.
5. Their husband or boyfriend depended upon them for money.
6. Someone made a mistake that created a temptation they could not resist.
7. They started taking minor amounts of money and covered the petty thefts by claiming they didn't know what was causing the $5 and $10 shortages. These petty thefts conditioned them to steal a large amount.
8. They stole the money because they thought they could throw suspicion on a new employee.
9. They don't know why they did it, they just did it.
10. They discovered the key to their personal vault in the main vault opened the personal vault of another teller, giving them the opportunity to steal that teller's money.
11. They needed an abortion.
12. They stole out of revenge because they didn't like the head teller or bank manager.
13. They stole because they felt the bank mistreated them.
14. They removed from another teller's cash drawer $1,000 as a joke to teach the teller not to leave her drawer unattended. They intended to tell the teller what they did and put the money back but then changed their mind.

EPILOGUE

Torture vs. The Intellectual Approach to Interrogation

This book was written before September 11, 2001. In Chapter Nine pertaining to "Spies, Hate Groups Members and Assassins," I mentioned the difficulty of interrogating ideologues. The intractability of the Muslim terrorist suspects during interrogation has become so frustrating that it has been suggested by some people that the suspects be sent to countries that employ torture in their interrogation procedure. For many years, I have experienced the frustration of interrogating suspects who believe that group protection is a virtue, and is not a vice to lie to a person in a position of authority. Terrorist suspects undoubtedly fail to cooperate out of fear of being ostracized and the fear of potential reprisals against themselves and their families. These beliefs are major roadblocks in breaking these suspects.

Despite the difficulty of the task, I don't believe that you need torture to break some of these suspects. I've worked in a multicultural city all my life, and it's been my experience that there are tough-minded people in every culture. I don't think the young Muslim terrorists are number one in that category. When you have multiple suspects, there is always the potential of someone talking because of the self-interest principle. Some suspects confess and cooperate to get a better deal, or because of a personal grievance against other suspects.

I believe there is an Achilles heel in the position of the terrorists. They have, in essence, defiled their own religion. That, in my opinion, makes them vulnerable to persuasive arguments based on history, religious concepts and moral philosophy. You can't break ideologues asking questions and sitting there like a human tape recorder. The best evidence that the terrorists are vulnerable to persuasive arguments is the fact that some demagogue, without putting a gun to their

147

head, talked them into terrorist activities. The demagogues achieve their goal by promising young terrorist recruits eternal recognition.

To counter the influence of terrorist leaders, the interrogator has to convince the young terrorist that he has been used. The suspect should be told that he is being sacrificed for the sole purpose of bene-fiting the person who talked him into the conspiracy to commit ter-rorist acts. This argument can change the attitude of the suspect, par-ticularly if the suspect already has a fear that he is being used. The sus-pect should be told that his leaders had led him into a cause that does not have the support of the vast majority of his own religion. He should be told that he has a choice between lying and identifying with corrupters of his own religion, or telling the truth and rejoining the vast majority of good people in his religion who are not the enemies of mankind.

One might question the effectiveness of verbal persuasion with those willing to commit suicidal attacks. The desire for self-annihila-tion is not unique to terrorists. Sigmund Freud believed that there is a death wish in many people. I've spent a lifetime interrogating peo-ple who, in essence, cut off their nose despite their face. The inter-rogator, to cope with the masochistic personality, has to tell the suspect precisely what he is doing to himself. The suspect should be told that he is not telling the truth because he is trying to hurt himself. It should be pointed out to the suspect that by doing that, he is guilty of the worst crime of all, a wasted life. To augment that argument, the sus-pect should be told that he has no guarantee that how he thinks at the present time will be the same way he thinks six months from now, or even years later. The suspect should be told that he will live to regret that he let a lie dictate his fate.

The secret to success with this type of suspect is to get him to a point where he interrogates himself. You let the suspect reflect upon what he has been told overnight or days if necessary. Giving a suspect time to think takes away the stigma that the interrogator is dictating to the suspect by demanding immediate cooperation. Many suspects who appear to be intractable confess during subsequent interrogation ses-sions. This tactic does not work if the interrogator does anything unprofessional, which would negate the persuasiveness of his argu-ment. The suspect has to feel comfortable with the interrogator. Terrorists generally expect to be mistreated, and when the mistreat-ment is not forthcoming, it can undermine their fixed beliefs. If the terrorist suspect is treated professionally, this increases their vulnerability to the intellectual approach in interrogation.

I have to acknowledge that torture is the most effective method for obtaining confessions. It is also the most effective method for obtaining confessions from the innocent. I've worked on enough miscarriage of justice cases to know the danger of abusive interrogation. The intellectual approach to interrogation is not a poor substitute for torture, nor is it construed by suspects as a weakness in the interrogator. The combination of patience and perseverance can get the job done with a lot more assurance that the information received is valid. As an interrogator, I have experienced personal satisfaction stringing words together, and convincing a person to tell me the truth. I can't imagine receiving the same degree of satisfaction using torture, and knowing I violated our nation's laws.

Charles C Thomas
PUBLISHER • LTD.

P.O. Box 19265
Springfield, IL 62794-9265

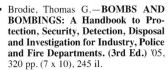
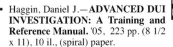

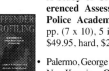
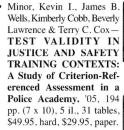
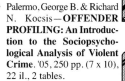

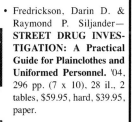
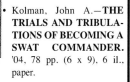